The Intuition Toolbox

KERRY!
THANK YOU
FOR YOUR
SUPPORT.
Paul White

The Intuition Toolbox

Paul Winter

Dedication

This dedication is directed to every young person whose life was radically changed by someone whom they never thanked. It happened to me. His name was William Cody. He was my ninth grade English teacher back in the Bronx. He got me into reading. He got the whole class into reading. My grades went from straight D's to straight A's. Without that change, I never would have gone to college. I never would have made it to California. I never would have written this book.

So here is what I would like to tell Mister Cody if I could: Forgive me for not telling you about my wonderful life, the life you made possible. Forgive me for not looking for you until it was too late to find you. You were a great teacher; you were outrageous and wonderfully inappropriate. We liked the inappropriate part the best, even though I guess, it eventually got you fired. I have tried to emulate your style and so help me, I've really learned the inappropriate part well. Still, I will never forget what you did for me.

So come on you young people. Don't *you* forget until it's too late. Find those special people and tell them what they mean to you.

Mister Cody, at this point, that is the best I can do.

Acknowledgements

My deepest thanks to a wonderful bunch of people. Whenever I think of all the hours they spent helping me, my spirit soars.

Audrey Knippen who took two weeks out of her vacation to teach me how to write and she edited this book a couple of times.

Coleen Garrity who has inspired me with the most unique but down home vocabulary I have even known and who hadn't edited in years, but still tackled my manuscript with gusto.

Dixie Pine who remains the best editor I ever worked with.

Karen Mueller who edited and played the role of the confused reader like only an engineer with a Ph.D. can.

Erin White who I hardly knew, but who agreed to edit my book purely out of the beauty of her heart.

Judy Glassing who, during her editing, found the most humor in my "creative" spelling.

Kao Yongvang who despite growing up in France in a household where they spoke Hmong, turned out to be an excellent editor.

Larry Castle who I never thought would find the time to edit, but did.

Larry Graves whose edits everybody loved.

My Mother who risked her life to bring me into this world and then risked her sanity to edit my manuscript.

Patty Ferrari the kindest editor to grace my pages.

Roi Gift who doggedly kept a positive attitude when I quit my career to write this book and whose editing was surprisingly insightful.

Susan Thomas who edited and supported me in innumerable ways during the writing of this book.

Table of Contents

Appendix B – Hypnotic Suggestions 182

Prologue

As far as the eye could see, the San Francisco bay was in turmoil. Wind whipped waves raced south looking for victims in small boats. Even on land the wind was so strong you had to lean into it. This was perfect weather for lunatic windsurfers. However, at the windsurfing site, the wind addicts were behaving oddly. Instead of frantically rigging storm sails and donning wet suits, then were walking circles in the grass with their heads bowed. They looked like so many monks heading to evening pray after excessively sampling the Abbey's finest product. Then, one windsurfer asked, "They're on a Toyota key chain?" The poor guy had lost his keys with his equipment still in his car. The grass was too long to easily find keys. I wanted to help, but I needed to walk unobstructed for my finding technique to work. After about five minutes, the owner of the keys encouraged them to give up and enjoy themselves.

When they returned to rigging their sails, I entered into a state of mind that you will soon learn about, raised my hand and pointed left then right. I started walking, continuing to point left and right, and followed the resultant feelings. After about 15 feet, I stopped, bent down, and picked up a ring of keys. The owner of the keys saw me pick up the keys and accused me of seeing him drop the keys and letting everybody waste their time looking for them. I told him that I had just finished writing a book about using intuition to do all sorts of things such as finding lost articles. His attitude changed completely and he asked if he could learn how to do it. I explained that it would take too much instruction for a casual conversation. but that I expected to have a book published soon and would let him know when it would be available. I added his name to a list I carried in my wallet. That was over ten years ago and the list is long gone. I hope they all forgive me.

Introduction

If you are attracted to this book, you have probably experienced intuition in your life. Perhaps you have had numerous experiences, but you found intuition unreliable. The problem is that people generally believe that using intuition is simply following what they feel. Fact, fiction, and fear, to only name the F's, can influence the way we feel but have nothing to do with our intuition. Accessing intuition is a skill like many others; it is difficult to learn without instruction, but nearly anyone can do it if they are taught a simple and effective method.

This book not only teaches such a method, but practicing this method will increase other abilities such as thinking clearly in pressure situations and following complex conversations. You may find that these additional benefits motivate you to access your intuition often and it will become a favorite tool for years to come.

A large part of using your intuition involves the removal of interfering feelings that lie just below your conscious thoughts. To keep this emotional residue from constantly building up, you will be shown different ways to develop peace of mind. To develop this peace of mind you must get control of your life. Therefore, this book contains tools for creating the best possible outcomes in your life. This book contains a whole box full of these tools.

Having tools that make things happen can create peace of mind only if you know yourself well. Therefore, you will be presented with some unusual ideas and asked for your opinions on each. It is hoped that you will disagree with some of these ideas because when disagreeing, a person examines their own beliefs and ideas to prove why they are right and the other is wrong. In this way your disagreements are more valuable than your agreements, therefore, many of the ideas in this book were chosen to be unconventional to encourage your disagreement. They cover various subjects which may not appear to have a direct relation to intuition. Their selection is designed to help you get to your deepest feelings for this is where intuition lies. The best part of this exploration is that deep down, past all the fears and guilt, there is a place of sheer bliss.

1 – *The Ultimate Value*

The L-1011 jetliner had dropped below one thousand feet on its final approach to Miami International Airport when the pilot noticed that the nose landing gear light was not indicating a normal down and locked position. Twice he tried to lower the gear as the jet continued its fateful descent. After the second unsuccessful attempt, the pilot radioed the control tower that he would have to abort the landing. Bringing the ship back up to two thousand feet, he engaged the auto pilot and began to investigate the landing gear problem. What the pilot didn't know was that the auto pilot had a problem of its own. The jet started to descend again.

Back in the cabin, some of the more experienced travelers knew something was wrong; the approach was taking too long and they were no longer flying toward the lights of Miami. Some passengers must have thought of the traveler's worst nightmare: being hijacked. Then, the sound of the landing gear could be heard coming down, not once, but twice. The image of a hijacking was quickly replaced by something even worse. Meanwhile, unnoticed by the pilot, the jet continued its descent.

When the jet passed below nine hundred feet, it disappeared from the radar screen in the control tower. A very worried controller picked up the phone and alerted the U.S. Coast Guard air and sea rescue station at Opa Locka, the busiest air and sea rescue station in the world. The senior duty officer on the other end rang the alarm, dispatched one helicopter, and started making calls to assemble the crew for a second helicopter. As the first helicopter lifted off, the officer aboard suspected that the mission was another false alarm. With clear weather and little wind, what could happen to a modern jet like the L-1011?

In the L-1011 cockpit the flight engineer tested the landing gear indicator and found that the bulb had burnt out. The co-pilot removed the indicator housing and replaced the bulb, but when he couldn't get the indicator housing back into the instrument panel, the pilot decided they would use a different method to verify that the landing gear was safe for landing. He sent the engineer down into the electronics bay under the cockpit where it would be possible to observe the landing gear position. Confident that the landing gear position would be verified, the pilot banked left to bring the plane back around toward Miami.

Suddenly the co-pilot noticed their altitude. The steep descent of the jet had gone undetected because both the pilot and co-pilot were preoccupied with trying to free the landing gear indicator housing. It had become jammed when the co-pilot had tried to put it in sideways. The co-pilot yelled an alarm and the pilot immediately pulled the control yoke back as much as he dared. The jet was flying dangerously slow so stalling was a real possibility. He pushed the throttles to maximum power in a desperate attempt to increase their airspeed for the climb out. The jet shuttered with the sudden response of the engines. Outside the window, the Everglades seemed to be reaching up to them., but the power of the engines was reassuring. The pilot silently thought, we are going to make it, we are going to make it.

The jet was still straightening out from the left course correction as the pilot started to bring its nose up. They needed hundreds of feet of altitude to bring the plane level because of the steep angle it had developed during its undetected descent. They almost made it.

When the L-1011 first hit the ground the impact was not severe and it lifted into the air again. The second impact was solid and devastating, ripping off all the landing gears and the left wing. The jet ripped a path through the tall grass and mud of the Everglades as it slid and spun out of control. The interior lights went out. Screams and the din of tortured metal filled the darkness. Suddenly a large crackling fireball raced down the length of the cabin. A blast of cold air and fuel assaulted the passengers as the fuselage started to break up. Passengers were thrown in every direction, but some remained strapped to their seats. Everything was happening so fast that a few people didn't realize that they had crashed. One man in first class who had been enjoying a double Scotch wondered what all the noise was about. Another man who apparently had blanked out during the actual crash snapped out of it and thought he had been in a normal landing until he realized that all of the jet forward of his seat was gone.

There was a high proportion of survivors because the jet had crashed into a part of the Everglades where the water was only a few feet deep, preventing the jet from sinking. Renee Shackelford was not among the survivors. So ended flight 401 on 29 December 1972.

Three weeks before the crash Louise Shackelford had a strong premonition and a day of depression that left her with the conviction that if anyone in her family traveled over the holidays, they would be in grave danger. She determined not to let anybody go anywhere during that time. Her daughter, Renee, had just started a new job in New York and did not believe that she could make it back to Miami for the holidays. Even so, the next time Louise talked to her daughter she insisted that Renee let her know immediately if she decided to come home. Louise intended to do all she could to discourage any plans her daughter might have to come home that month. However, at the last minute, Renee decided to surprise everyone. She didn't call; she just boarded the first available plane to Miami and flew to her death.

Louise had a strong and clear intuitive experience and, except for a lack of communication, she could have saved her daughter's life. Was it an isolated incident? Definitely not. Ask your friends if they know of similar examples of this kind of intuition – involuntary awareness not based on any previously received knowledge. You may be surprised; these incidents are quite common. Other books on intuition seem to be full of such examples, but if you find them among your acquaintances, you will realize just how common they really are. After your explorations, you are likely to ask yourself, why people don't use intuition more often. There are two reasons. The first reason is that many people believe that intuitive insights only come involuntarily. This is simply because people have not been taught how to access their intuition. The second reason is because the reliability of intuition has been unjustly degraded. This is due to the fact that people often fail to distinguish intuitive insight from a common and over-powering emotion – fear.

Fear or Intuition?

Have you ever experienced unexplainable dread or foreboding followed by some unexpected calamity? If you have, then you like Louise Shackelford, know the ultimate value of intuition. You could have prevented the calamity. Some of us have had forebodings, ignored them, and no calamity occurred. Was it just unfounded fear or did we unconsciously change something that averted the danger?

It is difficult to distinguish between an intuitive warning and an unfounded fear. Very few people can do it without instruction and practice. As children we are typically encouraged to ignore our intuition and use reasoning alone when making decisions. If we continue to ignore our intuitive abilities, we will waste an incredible skill.

Soon, you will learn a method for making the correct decision without pondering the known facts and puzzling over their interactions. You will learn to make the correct decision without the distraction of your ego or fear. This decision-making tool will have an advantage over the abilities demonstrated by Louise Shackelford. In Louise's care, intuition was invoked involuntarily. The tool you will be taught can be used voluntarily at any time no matter how important or insignificant the decision.

Although some people are more sensitive to their feelings than others, everyone has the ability to access their intuition. It is not just the sensitive person who can be highly intuitive. If you can quiet your fears, turn off your anxiety, and get in touch with yourself, you will experience intuition more strongly than a sensitive person who is worried or nervous.

Now that you know there is a specific intuition technique, you may want to know where it came from or how it was developed. That's a story that spans fifteen years.

2 – Searching for Intuition

A few months after I discovered the intuition technique, I asked myself, why me? When I looked at my life with that question in mind, things suddenly fell together. It seemed that I had been headed in a specific direction for a long time.

A Dreamer Is Born

Ever since I was very young, I have excelled in one particular area: daydreaming. In grade school, I became so engrossed in my dreams that I would unconsciously put my head down on my desk. This was a dangerous position because I could not see my teachers sneaking up on me. Their favorite technique was to slam their hand down on the desk right behind my head. For a few days after receiving these electrifying returns to reality, I would limit my dreaming to an upright posture, but the daydreaming rarely slackened. Teachers threatened to make me repeat each year, but I promised to work harder. They fell for it each year.

Machines have held a special, almost magical, attraction for me. Any machine that was fast and powerful or simply pretty could send me into a fine daydream. There were a few motorcycle types in my old neighborhood who were constantly working on their beautiful machines. These guys were a fascinating combination of tattoos, leather jackets and gentleness. Soon, I became convinced that working on motorcycle engines was the coolest thing possible, except for maybe working on jet fighters. Jets had to be way cooler. In my most favorite daydream, I was a jet fighter pilot. These daydreams were stimulated by one of my favorite toys, a small gray jet fighter. As I held it in my hand "flying" it through the air, it seemed to become bigger than life. At the time, I did not known how important gray colored fighters would become to me, but

19

that toy lived in my memory stronger than any other toy. I can still vividly see it rolling over and diving for the floor of a bedroom at least 20,000 feet below. When I would "land" the jet I would just sit and look at it while I imagined taking it apart to fix something. I was fascinated by what might be inside and imagined that I was the best at making the jets fly faster and better than anyone else. At the time I thought pilots worked on their jets just like the motorcycle riders worked on their bikes.

When I was able to handle a screwdriver, I became skilled at taking things apart and figuring out how they worked. This was sometimes annoying to my father who wasn't fond of putting his radio back together just to hear the news. My mother confused my interest with the ability to fix things. She started bringing me her friends broken toasters and clocks. I would take then apart to see how they worked. As I checked out what did what, I sometimes noticed why they weren't working. Before I knew it, I *could* fix things. As I grew older, my dreams changed to fast cars and girls, but the image of that gray toy fighter returned from time to time. I thought it was just a memory that got stuck in my mind like a song with a strong hook, but it turned out to be much more.

I didn't enjoy school, but I applied to a few colleges to keep my parents happy. I applied as an engineering student because I had some idea of what I was doing in math class. To my great surprise, I was accepted to CCNY, a tuition free university with a well respected engineering college. College was a drag, but every summer I had an excellent opportunity to hone my daydreaming skills. I worked as a lifeguard on a beach that had to be covered from 8:00 AM to 8:00PM. If I had the early watch on overcast days, I wouldn't see anyone for hours. Sitting in a high chair with nothing to do and nothing to look at but endless water drove some of the other lifeguards crazy. Not me – I loved it – I was getting paid for daydreaming. By then, I had realized that becoming a jet-fighter pilot was not for me. It was the time of war protests and throwing eggs at ROTC students. But, I stilled dreamed of working on jets. I had learned the term field engineer and thought that the coolest job would be as a civilian troubleshooter who was called by the Air Force to fix the jets that had special problems. When I learned about this job, I was already three years into college and very pleased to discover that I had been studying the right subjects all along. My beach days were filled with daydreams of being driven up to a torn-apart jet fighter with a bunch of air force types standing around scratching their heads. A few minutes later I would solve the problem to the accompaniment of muttered curses.

Don't get me wrong, working on the beach was not always full of daydreams. When people came, they came in droves. It seemed half of them couldn't swim five feet. Saving people scared some of the other lifeguards, it even put one in the hospital, but I was on the swimming and waterpolo teams at my college. We played waterpolo against schools like Army and Yale where everybody was twice my size. This made saving people easy, even if I had to pull out two people by myself (people tend to drown in pairs – arms wrapped around the other in blind panic). We didn't have any buoys for pulling people in. Sometimes I would just let them grab me so I had both hands and arms free for swimming. I would grab some air if I got the chance. If I didn't, I would just go under water; people almost always let go when you start to go down. Only once did I see a victim not let go. The result was that one of my lifeguard mates woke up in the hospital. When I left that job, I had the satisfaction of knowing that I had saved more than 70 people and that no one had died while I was on duty. I started out in the working world full of confidence and positive images because of those summers. That confidence may have been responsible for the wonderful life I have had or maybe it was the day dreaming.

Before I explain the uses for day dreaming, I would like to pass on a point about saving people because it is usually done incorrectly on TV and the old life guard in me can't allow it. If you pull a person out of the water who has stopped breathing, give them a hip-roll:

1. Turn them on their stomach with their head downhill.
2. If you can, get another person to help this second step: work your hands under the victims hip's.
3. Lift their hips as high as you can. This causes water to run out of their lungs.

Mouth-to-mouth is useless if a person's lungs are full of water. Draining the water out of a person's lungs is usually enough to stimulate breathing. Mouth-to-mouth with the lungs full of water usually forces air into a person's stomach and you wind up with their lunch in your face. If they haven't started breathing after the hip-role they may have closed their air-passage when they went under and managed to keep it closed even after they passed out although such presence of mind while drowning is rare. In this case mouth-to-mouth should stimulate breathing, but still look out for launching lunches.

Disaster Strikes, I Dream On

Right before I finished school, massive layoffs occurred in the Aerospace industry. Engineers were driving taxi cabs. My school chums were depressed, but it didn't seem to affect my spirits. My favorite daydream was so close to becoming reality that I couldn't stop dreaming it. Failure didn't even occur to me. I set my sights on one company. While my friends sent out hundreds of letters to every company that ever hired an engineer, I sent one letter. It went to the Hughes Aircraft company. Even though Hughes was 3,000 miles away, I got an interview. It definitely wasn't my grades – I graduated by the skin of my teeth. I believe getting that interview had to do with something more interesting. Before I finished school a friend taught me something that seemed to have a mind-over-matter effect on events. I directed this tool at getting the Hughes Aircraft job. After that success, I continued to use it whenever I wanted to change jobs. The last position I accepted took me one week to find.

There are three such mind-over-matter tools described later in this book. To teach them so early and without introductory explanations might bias you against them. These types of tools appear to have little to do with intuition, but they allow you to have the control over your life that promotes the peace of mind that helps you to get in touch with your intuition.

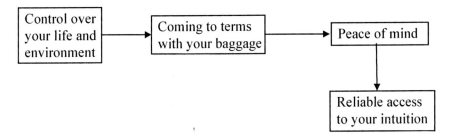

Figure 1. Simplified Path to Reliable Intuition

Two weeks after the interview, I received an acceptance letter from Hughes Aircraft. The job started with a six month training course. The course taught the inner workings of the most complicated jet fighter system Hughes Aircraft every produced. I was so fascinated that I could remember everything taught despite the eight hours of daily instruction. It was serious business and we had periodic tests. For the first time in my life, I knew the subject so well that I didn't need to study and still aced the tests. After years of exam anxiety and poor grades I was an A student without even trying. I was in heaven.

One morning before the instructor arrived, the other students started comparing how many letters they had written to get the job. The frustration in their voices varied with the numbers, between 200 and 350 letters each. One of the guys started talking about working in a body shop in Minnesota with ice dripping in his eyes, but after this brief distraction from the question at hand, they turned to me. "Well?" they said as I inched my way towards the door. I decided a brief reply without an explanation would assist my departure, "One." As I flew down the hallway the cheer went up, "Get him!" At last, a target for their frustration.

Before I knew it, I was working on real fighters. It was a couple of years before I actually became the field engineer the Air Force called on when they couldn't fix a jet, but it was inevitable. Of course, life doesn't always resemble one's dreams. I remember cold West German nights walking down the flightline (the area where the jets are parked) with the fog and the blue lights competing to hide or illuminate the maze of taxi ways that lay before me. I would be in a rush to find some obscure revetment (cold, concrete bunkers where some jets are placed) before the Air Force team finishes and gets *driven* back. Oh, there they go. Of course it isn't always cold on a flightline. I remember one sunny day in the Philippines; it was an even 90 degrees in the shade. Twenty fighter planes, all facing in different directions, were firing up at the same time to join some mass exercise. Once the jets started pulling out and turning around to taxi out, you couldn't hide from the searing jet exhausts. One of the flightline troops was walking around with a hot-dog on a stick and claiming that it was almost done. The heat on the flightline had cooked it.

Wouldn't it be wonderful if you could figure out an approach to problems that allowed you the same success as I had with my dream? Especially if you were more careful with what you dreamed for? Actually, I loved my work as a field engineer and it gave me the initial motivation to find something beyond logic and knowledge to help me make decisions. That job was clearly confirmation of the power of dreaming. One evening just past sunset, I made this heart-warming discovery: I was walking up to an F-15 (my favorite fighter) that was sitting alone at the end of the flightline. The belly tank which the F-15 usually flies with, had been removed giving the jet a sleeker profile. The sky was a beautiful deep blue and the heat of the day had been replaced by a cool breeze. As I looked at the F-15, I was struck with an amazing recognition. Perhaps it was the flat light and the angle that made the jet seem smoother, more plastic, but I finally realized that the jet I had grown to know and love the most looked just like the toy I had loved so many years before.

The Search Begins

I worked on my own, usually overseas, with no one else to blame if I made a mistake. I was highly motivated to do a good job and make the right decisions, because I worked and played with the people who flew the jets. If I messed up, it would be hard to find someone I could look in the eye and still feel good about myself. It was not just pride. If the equipment didn't work correctly, thousands of dollars worth of time and effort would be wasted in just one flight. I knew I had good analytical skills; I was organized and thorough, I did not rush, and I collected as much information as possible before making decisions. Still, my decisions were not always correct.

I examined the decisions I had made that didn't turn out well. Most of them seemed to have been the right choices based on the available facts. However, the available information was incomplete. Making decisions based on the available facts had a terrible flaw. Just one of the missing facts could indicate a completely different decision. There had to be a better way to make decisions. I had no idea whom to turn to or where to go for help, but help was soon to arrive.

On one of my earlier assignments, I went to work with the Chinese (ROC) Air Force on an air base that also had a US Air Force fighter squadron. I was allowed to use the US Air Force officers' club and stay at the visiting officers' quarters until I found my own place off base. One night I decided to eat at the officers' club.

I walked into an almost deserted dining room. There was one man there, sitting alone near the middle of the room. I went over and asked if he would mind some company; it seemed like the thing to do since the place was so empty. He turned out to be a very interesting pilot with such great flying stories that I thought I was going to get air sick. He talked about flying and philosophy and the strange country we were in. I noticed he was of high rank, but pilots like to be casual, so I talked to him like he was just one of the guys. I think my naiveté humored him.

I had not introduced myself when we first had met. Sometimes I don't exchange names with someone until we are about to part. It is actually easier to remember someone's name this way. So when we were about to leave I told him my name and what a pleasure it had been to meet him. He shook my hand and said that he was Colonel so and so, the base commander, and that I should drop by his office if there was anything I needed.

I could hardly believe my ears. He looked so young. But I blessed my luck and made sure to "drop by" the next day. Although we never became close friends, he did invite me to a few social gatherings, and we had some good conversations. He had many unusual ideas that made a lot of sense. I was surprised to discover that, although he had risen rapidly in the air force, he wasn't a driven workaholic. From the adventures he related to me, he played much more than most men his age. One evening I finally asked him how he ran an air force base and had time to do all the other things he talked about. He answered without hesitation: "a good gut feel." He went further to explain that there is never enough information to really nail down a hard decision so he just "shot from the hip". I knew exactly what he meant about hard decisions, but I hadn't used my hips since dancing the Twist. Though I tried to understand the actual method, he failed to elaborate more than to say, "Go with what you feel."

I tried to do what the Colonel said and feel with my gut, but when I tried to use my gut to make a decision it didn't tell me anything except "I'm hungry". I thought that might mean that I would get the message if I would go and eat something. I gained 5 pounds – no messages.

I decided to learn as much as I could about this gut feel concept and try to figure out how it interacted with the decision-making process. I was a welcome visitor to the Colonel's office and so would sometimes drop by to tell him how things were going on the Chinese side of the base, and then stay around to shoot the breeze. I enjoyed talking to him, but wasn't sure I was learning anything about the gut feel.

During these visits, the only thing I noted out of the ordinary was how relaxed he seemed, and how he would quiet down anybody who entered the room excited. We would often be interrupted by someone who needed a quick decision. He would say, "come on now, just relax a minute we'll fix 'er up." When it came time for him to solve a problem or make the decision, he would always do the same thing. He would lean way back in his chair, lock his fingers behind his head, and take a deep breath, just like he had all the time in the world.

I would think, how can a man who seems to be taking his time about everything, get anything done? When I thought about it some more, I realized that he didn't actually spend that much time making the decision. He rarely asked for more information than his visitor volunteered, and he didn't encourage any discussion. He just stretched, relaxed, and talked slowly. There it was, in front of me all the time – relax, calm yourself. No wonder I couldn't get a gut feeling; the shop I worked in was a madhouse and I was the head maniac.

So I had one piece of the puzzle: relax, take it slow. I tried applying this relaxed attitude to my own decision-making, but found that there were still too many feelings flying around inside me. I didn't know which one was my gut feel and which one was guilt from not writing my mother. I finally gave up. I knew that I could learn to use intuition only if I could learn a step by step technique that would get past my normal jumble of feelings.

Looking back it is clear to me that the Colonel was born with great intuitive talent. It was second nature for him to eliminate the jumble of feelings that get in the way of intuition. But, doing this is not like swinging a bat. It can't be shown to the student; no images are available. This makes the manipulation or feelings very hard to teach. Based on the term "gut feel" it seems that the Colonel used feelings, but he couldn't teach his method beyond this description. I had to learn how to eliminate my interfering feelings without his help.

A few years went by and I started to meditate. Through meditation I developed increased sensitivity to my inner feelings and my physical health. This sensitivity allowed me to feel the onset of illness very early, so I could take steps to prevent getting sick when the invaders were at their weakest and I was at my strongest. This was so effective that it encouraged me to find other ways to use this sensitivity.

The Discovery

We all have a need to create. My need pushes me to my work bench where I find myself making terribly useful things like a remote control for the backyard sprinkler. No sense walking five feet out the door, when in just three hours I can build a remote. But, I digress. One evening, I had to repeatedly perform an operation for a precise amount of time, which varied from five to ten seconds. If I went too far I could go back, but it was a real bother. I decided to try applying my increased sensitivity in order to "feel" the right moment to stop. At first I wasn't able to feel anything. Then I decided to modify a problem solving technique that I had developed for technical problem solving and apply it to helping me stop at the right moment.

The first time I tried this, I stopped at exactly the right place. The same thing happened the next time and the next. Then, I sat down with my mouth open for about ten minutes and considered the implications of what I had discovered.

The technique was so easy to use that I eventually started calling it a tool. I applied this tool to different situations that also had an exact point in time when the action had to be stopped. *It worked every time.* And it only needed slight modifications to be used with yes or no decisions. I was making more tools. I wondered if I could teach my friends who had trouble making decisions. I was confident that the tools could be easily taught because of their step by step nature. My only concern was the level of sensitivity that people need in order to feel the right moment. I initially avoided this problem by starting with a friend who also meditated. She was able to accept the concepts involved, or at least suspend her skepticism, for the duration of the experiment. Then I taught her the steps that she would need to practice. She learned the steps quickly and agreed to practice the problem solving procedure consistently until she felt ready to use the intuition technique.

A couple of weeks later my friend called. "You'll never guess what happened!" she exclaimed. "I was at a baby shower, and they played a game where everybody tries to cut a piece of string to the same size as the expectant mother's waistline. I got into that state of mind you taught me, then took the string, and before I cut it, I applied your intuition technique. When everybody tried their piece of string, nobody's came anywhere near except mine. Mine was exactly the right length!" Right then I knew that my intuition technique could be taught to others. In retrospect, I realize that they were fairly easy to learn for the right person and starting calling them intuition tools to make them appear more user-friendly.

What was especially encouraging was that I had never taught her how to measure string using intuition, although I had taught her a tool for measuring ingredients for cooking. She had developed the string measuring application herself. This verified an old theory of mine: what works best is the idea you come up with yourself. Since her first success with her own application, she has developed other applications.

The next person I taught my tools to did not meditate. She had a simple home life, but as an emergency veterinarian her work was full of the pressure of life and death situations. She is a confident and competent person and has learned to calm herself, despite squished pets and frantic pet owners, in order to perform her job without becoming a total wreck. She was able to learn the intuition tools quickly. Perhaps the calming skills that she learned at work aided her in successfully learning and using my tools with little effort. It started to become clear that the ability to calm oneself helps a great deal when trying to access your intuition.

How To Approach the Tools

I had been meditating for many years when I discovered the tools that allowed easy access to intuition. Since then I have successfully taught them to others who also meditated, and some who did not. Those who meditated could more easily develop a state of mind that is quiet enough for them to come in contact with their deeper feelings. So, if you have meditated before, this would be a good time to take it up again. If you never meditated, this would be a good time to start. Some meditations are included in this book, but most meditation methods will work.

There are two skills required for accessing your intuition:

♦   An ability to quiet your fears and anxiety
♦   An ability to get in touch with your deeper feelings

To learn how to access your intuition, you will be taught a number of initial tools that, when used in combination with each other, form a major part of the intuition technique. If you start using these initial tools as soon as they are revealed to you, you will learn the final intuition technique more easily. Using the tools has its own rewards – helping you solve problems, thinking more clearly in pressure situations, and enjoying things more intensely. When you reach the intuition technique your success will be assured because of the confidence you developed from using the initial tools.

As you read this book, you may recognize sections designed to help you know yourself better, get control of your life, and obtain *peace of mind.* This will allow you closer contact with your deeper feelings. Some of you have already achieved this close contact. In which case it is hoped that you will find some unusual ideas in this book that cause you to realize some of your own opinions which you were not previously aware. Realizing these previously unknown opinions of yours is most likely to occur if you disagree with these unusual ideas. Disagreeing causes a person to examine their opinions as a defense and verification mechanism. This examination may help you to learn more about yourself.

Why All The Strange and Different Ideas

I learned the value of strange and different ideas during the eight years I worked for Hughes Aircraft. Most of that time I lived overseas. I would live in each country for a year or two and then move on. During my time off, I experienced cultures that were vastly different from my own. I say "experience" rather than "understand" because understanding would have been a full time job.

Through driving around and casual exploration I observed that people in different countries do almost everything differently. They build differently, they wait in line differently, they eat differently, they strike matches differently. . . most importantly, they think differently and have a different sense of values. I would contemplate these differences and try to determine what made these people behave and think differently. Very quickly I came to an impasse in my deliberations due to a lack of detailed historical and cultural knowledge. What automatically happened at this point was that I would begin to consider the basis of my own behavior and thoughts on that subject. This was much easier since I had plenty of background knowledge concerning my own culture and sense of values. However, without the people in those far away places showing me different approaches, I would never have examined myself or my culture under the light such a different light

I soon realized that my ideas and goals were not the result of simply being a man with a propensity towards free-thinking. To a large extent, my ideas were the result of a set of previously unknown influences. The more strange and different things I observed about people in foreign countries, the more I examined the person I had become and what had influenced me. The results of these examinations were so valuable that I wrote them down, and that made all the difference. I learned what parts of myself were really my own and what parts were the result of cultural and social influences. I not only learned about myself and the society I grew up in, but discovered motivations and tools for the changes I wished to make in myself.

Soon I will present ideas and concepts which may seem strange and different from mainstream thinking. Consider them a trip to a foreign country. It is not important that you become a native and agree with them; diversity is strength. However, it is essential that you carefully deliberate on why you agree or disagree. Through these deliberations you will discover and examine your own values and motivations. In this manner, you will increase your understanding of yourself, and therefore increase your self-awareness. It is this self-awareness that inevitably leads to contact with your deeper feelings, wherein lies your intuition. The greatest aid to your deliberations is to write down why you agree or disagree with an idea and what you learned from that deliberation. If no answer comes, simply start writing anything you know on the subject. You may be surprised how your mind will make your opinions known when you go through the mechanical process of writing things down. Also, writing can help you remember your discoveries and prevent you from repeating character building ordeals.

Emotional Interference – Baggage

Understanding a couple of basic concepts about your feeling will aid you in accessing your intuition. You must feel calm and secure to access your intuition. Disquieting feelings such as those caused by emotions like hate, frustration, and anger must be properly dealt with to prevent their interference. You will be taught tools that can temporarily quiet these interfering feelings. This type of quieting is no substitute for permanently taking care of the problems that caused the interfering feelings in the first place. Quieting feelings is a potentially dangerous procedure. You will learn more about these dangers and how to avoid them shortly.

Positive feelings usually make a person feel more secure and relaxed, and this enhances contact with one's intuition. However, excessively strong positive feelings can also interfere with intuition. It is very easy to tone down these feelings with something depressing such as the front page of any newspaper.

There are other, more subtle emotions that can cause disquieting feelings besides fear, hate, and anger. These subtle emotions cause feelings which often lie just below your consciousness, as does your intuition. Among these subtle emotions are guilt, regret, and resentment. In order to access your intuition, the feelings caused by these subtle emotions must also be removed. Just as with strong negative feelings, the removal of these feelings on a temporary basis is not a substitute for dealing with the problems that caused them. Even these subtle feelings will return again and again until you work through them. Often people carry these feelings for a long time, thus the term "emotional baggage." Dealing properly with emotional baggage usually requires a specific approach for each problem. However, there is one useful approach that works for a number of issues: increase your understanding of the problem by communicating with yourself and the other concerned parties. A most effective way to communicate with yourself is to write about the problem. Face-to-face is the best way to communicate with others. Whatever the method, communication is the key. This may sound simple, but often communication is the most difficult part of solving the problem. Once communication is established the other parts of the problem seem to take care of themselves.

To help you deal with interfering feelings, you will be taught how to make yourself more aware of your feelings. Initially, this may be an unpleasant experience. Many people with unresolved issues avoid their feelings because these issues cause their feelings to be unpleasant. This is such a prevalent situation that many people find pleasure with anything that distracts them from their feelings. If you are a person with unresolved issues that cause unpleasant feelings, one of two things is likely to happen when you learn to become more aware of your feelings:

1. The discomfort you feel as a result of getting closer to your feelings will make you resist proceeding any further with this book.

2. The discomfort you feel will give you motivation to deal with your unresolved issues and change the way you respond to problems. Eventually this will reduce the accumulation of interfering feelings. When you have accomplished this, the experience of getting closer to your deeper feelings will start to become pleasurable.

As you get closer to dealing with your emotional baggage, realize that these are disturbing subjects; you avoided them because of that aspect. Feelings may come to the forefront with unpleasant strength. You are strongly advised to seek professional help if confronting these feelings becomes too difficult or disturbing. If you succeed in dealing with your emotional baggage you will be well on your way to peace of mind.

Peace of Mind and Self-discovery

This book is designed, in a slightly devious way, to encourage self-discovery while presenting ideas that promote peace of mind. The most pleasant assistance you can develop to facilitate this self-discovery process will be friendships with caring and forthright people. If you don't have enough of these, seek out people who will take the time to really know you and be kind enough to tell you about yourself in a supportive manner. Without good friends, finding peace of mind can be impossible and no way near as much fun. Now that you have this requirement, perhaps you have a way to approach potential friends: "I'm reading this book that *requires* I make new friends, it describes the type of people I should look for, and you appear to be such a person." People are often interested in the image they present to others, therefore, mentioning that image may encourage them enough to overcome their fear and start a conversation.

The method of promoting peace of mind used in this book has many side benefits. One of the tools taught will encourage you to occasionally observe yourself and the things around you in a certain way. This tool, called Center of Mind, is designed to improve your awareness, but it also improves concentration, comprehension and memory. As you increase your awareness, you may start paying more attention to, and therefore be more affected by, things in your physical environment. This is a significant step towards improving the way you feel. As you begin to notice how your surroundings affect the way you feel, you can make changes to your surroundings that will cause you to feel better.

Intuition may sound that it is only for people who can exercise strong control over their emotions and thus obtain peace of mind. This is not true. People who try to constantly control their emotions will usually collect a lot of interfering feelings. If you work through your emotions, such as allowing them expression rather than trying to constantly control them, you are more likely to achieve peace of mind. Resist the temptation to present an impressive image of total control by denying that you have suppressed feelings. The more certain you think you are of your emotional equilibrium, the more difficult it will be to get at the feelings you have suppressed.

Losing Our Intuition

Despite the stories of intuition that everyone seems to have, few parents encourage their children to trust and use their intuition. In school we are taught to think things through, rather than use our intuition. Because of this, it is probably a bad idea for the average person to attempt to use intuition since they have not been trained to recognize what intuition is and what it is not.   The picnic was in a meadow surrounded by lush woods and gently rolling hills. The beauty of nature was unspoiled by any signs of civilization, but Carol didn't appreciate anything about it. Her most recent complaint concerned the lack of plumbing. Her mother said, "if you have to go, go behind those bushes over there,"

When Carol went behind the bushes she thought that everybody could see her, so she decided to walk further away. Shortly, she came upon a trail that she followed until she felt she was sure that no one at the picnic could see her. Then she realized that anybody could come down the trail and see her if she didn't move away from the trail. She walked into the woods.

By the time Carol found a spot that satisfied her, she was half way to the next state. When she finally finished, she looked in the direction she had come from, but the forest did not look familiar. She looked in the direction that she had been going and of course it looked much more familiar because that was what she saw as she approached her current location. Foolishly, she decided to go in the direction that looked more familiar.

In a few minutes she realized that she was lost. At this point Carol made her fateful decision. She followed her feelings of fear, which were frantically telling her to keep going and find her family. If she had stopped to think she might have realized that she should have stayed put. Her family would have come looking for her and easily found her: Instead, by continuing to walk, she was getting further and further away from them and reducing their chances of finding her.

After walking for what seemed like a very long time, Carol decided that finding a road or anything would be a lot easier than finding that dumb old picnic area. Recalling her girl scout training (when lost in the woods, head downhill), she stopped paying any attention to direction and only looked for downhill slopes. Carol's luck had not changed. She had crossed a ridge, downhill was now away from everything.

The further Carol walked, the more afraid she became, and the more afraid she became, the faster she walked. The rolling hills of the forest made for limited visibility, but the tall pine trees with few lower branches and sparse underbrush made walking easy. As an eleven-year-old in good shape, she made great time. After continuous walking and some running, Carol was three miles away from her family and still heading away from civilization. It was 4 o'clock in the afternoon with perhaps three hours of daylight left.

The hours of walking and the fear of being lost started to take their toll on Carol's energy. She felt exhausted and looked for a good place to rest. She found a place that was too good. A fallen tree had rolled up against another, making a comfortable nook that fit Carol perfectly. The descending sun fell right on her. Exhausted and warm, she fell asleep.

Carol awoke shivering. It was almost dark. At first she thought she was at home in bed but then she remembered her predicament and started to cry. The forest looked much more frightening now that it was mostly shadow. She was too frightened to walk any further. Now that she wasn't walking and making her own noise she could hear all the sounds of the forest. She imagined the sound of a bird hopping through the underbrush as a wolf following her trail. She was too cold and afraid to sleep now and could only look out at the darkening forest with increasing terror. Just before midnight a new terror was presented to Carol. Something was moving in the darkness. Something was coming towards her.

When Carol's family couldn't find her they contacted the rangers. The rangers searched until dusk without finding a sign of Carol. The nights that week were very cold. Time had become the enemy. They called a tracker who had dogs that carried a special little pack on their backs. When the tracker arrived he let the dogs smell Carol's sweater and let them loose. They disappeared into the woods.

Back in the woods Carol could now just make out the "something". It was big and coming nearer and nearer. Then she heard a voice. It was a human voice, but she couldn't understand the words. Then the something was right in front of her and she could tell that is was just a dog, but the voice was coming from the dog. A talking dog had found her. And now she could understand the voice, "If you hear this recording, press the red button on the dog's back". Carol looked at the small pack on the dogs back and pushed the button that was glowing a dull red. Back at the tracker's truck, an alarm went off. The tracker looked at a digital read out. It told him the direction and distance to the dog those button was pushed. A quick look at the map and he found a logging road half a mile from the spot. Everyone piled into the truck. Within an hour Carol and her family were rediscovering how much they loved each other.

The next day, after the joy of being reunited had worn off, Carol's father questioned the young girl. "When did you realize you were lost?" he demanded.

"When I couldn't find the trail," Carol answered.

"Right then you should have stayed where you were. We could have found you so easily."

"Yes, but I was so scared, and I felt that I had to keep looking for you."

"Now young lady," her father said, "when you have an important decision to make, you must think about the facts and not go with just what you feel. Remember that and terrible things like this will not happen to you."

The lesson that Carol will remember from her night of terror will be: do not follow your feelings when making decisions; analyze the facts. Furthermore, since no one is likely to teach her the distinction between following feelings (such as responding to her fear) and following intuition, Carol has learned to disregard her intuition.

When you make a decision there are many feelings that can influence you. Some may have to do with the present situation, and others may be the result of unresolved issues from the past that were similar to the present problem. These feelings can be much stronger than your intuition, but when most people decide to go with their intuition they don't try to separate out the rest of their feelings. Sometimes, during the examination of a disastrous decision like Carol's, intuition takes the blame for the mistakes that were actually based on our less enlightened feelings. In Carol's case, in was fear.

For simple situations, using analysis to make the decision is a sound practice and it is easy to defend. However, more for complex situations, facts form a poor decision-making ally. This is when our upbringing and traditional education fail us.

Children are born with powerful intuition, but it is neglected by education and suppressed by incidents like Carol's where they are discouraged from using their intuition. After years of disuse, our intuitive skills decrease. These skills can be gradually awakened with a little bit of training.

Training Your Intuition

After you are taught the technique to access your intuition you will be encouraged to use it often. You will start with simple everyday decisions. They will be your "low risk training." When you have developed your confidence through low risk training, you can apply the technique to serious decisions.

Traditionally, your ability to make decisions depends on your ability to analyze the facts. Unfortunately, there are rarely enough facts to ensure a correct decision. Sometimes there are plenty of facts but they are so complicated and interdependent that they are misleading. Sometimes all the information seems to be available, but the indicated decision is wrong because some facts were missing. Because of these situations accomplishments are obstructed. The application of reliable intuition can improve your decision-making ability and save the time usually spent analyzing the facts.

If you make many important decisions in the course of a day, then you have an advantage. Once you have learned the intuitive decision-making tools, you can experiment with and evaluate your intuition without any risk. After making a decision in your usual way, you can use the tools to see what your intuition tells you. Then proceed based on your original decision obtained in your usual way. Later, when things progress to a point where review is possible, you can see how accurate your intuition would have been. I know that my intuition is more accurate than my decisions based on analysis because for years I have been experimenting with this procedure.

Intuition At Work

Shortly after developing my intuition technique it became necessary that I locate a manufacturer for a particular type of radio. It was important that the manufacturer had already produced something similar to the requirements of my project. From one trade publication I found 20 radio manufacturers that might meet our needs. I knew I would eventually have to get bids from each of those 20 manufacturers in order to demonstrate to our customer that we had done sufficient research to find the best radio, but time was important. If I managed to contact the best manufacturer early, I would be able to get them going sooner and save a week. (The calls would take a long time and I only had time for three or four a day.) I went to my boss with the list of manufacturers and asked if he had any idea who might best suit our needs. He didn't. Using a variation of the intuition technique, I pointed to a particular manufacturer and said, "I feel this one." I called that manufacturer first, got them started, and continued calling the other manufacturers. When I finished collecting the results, it was clear that the manufacturer I picked first was the best choice.

You may believe that you lack sufficient self-awareness to sense your intuition. Let me tell you about Tom, one of my dumbest friends. I know how dumb he really is because we lived together. One of my more discerning and eloquent friends refers to poor Tom as "beautifully stupid". Tom is a classic fetch mutt. He will fetch a ball, a Frisbee, a stick, a log, a rock. Anything you can throw, Tom will carry, drag, or push back to you. Furthermore, if you don't take it from him as soon as he brings it back, he will place it in your hand, your lap, your drink, or wherever he thinks it will get the most attention.

If Tom is fetching a ball on an uphill, he will get a head start on the next throw by dropping the ball on the ground ten or twenty feet in front of me. This starts the ball rolling down to where I am standing. Tom must think it is very important that the ball hit my foot to be sure that it gets my attention. The ball always hits my foot. It does not matter how bumpy the ground is. I have seen the ball go three feet off course and I think, "you missed me this time Tom," but damned if it doesn't curve back and hit my foot. It's not analysis of the bumpy ground. Tom intuitively knows where to place the ball to successfully hit my foot. If a dog who thinks lettuce is good food can use his intuition with such accuracy, you can surely learn to use yours. However, there are some people who will love to tell you that you can't.

The Contrarians

Or Strange Idea #1

Why is it that when an idea cannot be "proven," it is considered fair game, to be hunted down and killed as if doing so were good sport? Isn't an idea worthwhile if it can simply be put to good use? What do people gain when they can find fault with something? The answers to these questions will help you deal with your own doubts, but the answers are easy to forget. The extra effort to keep them in mind will fortify your own intuition.

When I look back on the times when I have discussed intuition with different people, I recall that the scientific types were the least receptive. Some have even become belligerent in their insistence upon proof. The only proof these people would consider would be repeated and consistent occurrences in their own lives. However, they would not be willing to go through the training that intuition usually requires since their attitude would prevent them from trying something without first seeing proof that it worked. I have never been able to get anywhere with these people except around and around, which is something I think they like. Is this you?

Formal scientific curriculum teaches that an idea (they call it a hypothesis) has to be demonstrated by repeatable experimentation or it is considered unproven. This is the definition of scientific proof. That requirement would make most of the important things I have learned in my life invalid. It would also free every murderer in jail. You can't repeatedly have someone murdered in order to confirm who did it. Scientific proof rarely applies to living your life; it belongs in the lab. You cannot apply scientific thinking to the way you live and expect to progress very quickly. If you let intuition guide your progress, you will become involved in an exciting adventure. If you let science be your guide, you will have more time to sleep, but that's about all.

Another group that seems to have a negative attitude towards intuition as a valid decision-making tool is the academicians. By academicians I refer to the professors and educators of our great institutions of higher learning who have spent thousands of hours developing their knowledge through research and study or, in other words, collecting facts. These people can't base decisions on feelings instead of information. That would leave them open to ridicule. They fear ridicule because it is still used as a tool to educate.

The academicians have given universities the exalted position of sole purveyors of knowledge. They believe that knowledge is only valid if it is sanctioned by a university. The discoveries of individuals outside of the university are looked upon with disdain and are therefore prevented from reaching people who need them. This is a terrible thing, but it has been happening for centuries and it continues to happen.

I have a friend whose father is a board-certified Obstetrician-Gynecologist. He is well respected by his colleagues and has been called as an expert witness for numerous legal proceedings. While working in a geographically isolated area he had the opportunity to observe a group of women who had a higher than average rate of toxemia. Toxemia is a serious disorder that occurs in five to seven percent of pregnancies in the United States, and is a prevalent cause of death for pregnant women and their babies. Currently, there is no effective cure except early termination of the pregnancies, nor is there a known preventative.

Through observations of severe toxemia cases in this area this doctor noticed similarities to beriberi which is caused by a vitamin B deficiency. He concluded that vitamin B1 might prevent toxemia. Working in this area for one year was a great opportunity to test the effectiveness of this simple preventative. Since vitamin B1 had no established side effects, 400 pregnant women were orally given 100 milligrams of the vitamin daily, started by the twelfth week of pregnancy. With a group of this size, even in the United States, the absolute minimum expected number of toxemia cases would be 20. The actual number of cases in his study was zero. Zero.

With such startling results you would think this treatment would be welcomed with open arms by the medical community. Wrong. This doctor is a practitioner; he is not a research doctor at a university. For years this distinction has prevented him from publishing his findings in medical journals and from having his treatments accepted at local hospitals.

He has developed other effective treatments for difficult disorders, such as arthritis, MS, lupus, and premenstrual syndrome, but has run into the same professorial barricade. He has contacted the universities where the research is being done but they are not interested in the case histories he is willing to produce. Their attitude seems to be that, only doctors who work in a university can have any credible knowledge to contribute. This seems incredible considering how isolated research doctors are from real practice.

So it seems that scientists and academicians, by the nature of their occupation and their fear of being wrong, are most likely to accept only knowledge that can be absolutely proven or is backed up by evidence from their own "club". This same attitude prevents them from supporting concepts like intuition. This is most unfortunate since scientists and educators strongly influence the public's acceptance of ideas. Even more unfortunate is that educators decide what will be taught in our schools.

Educators tend toward ideas based on the values and experiences of an educator and not, for example, on experiences of a business manager.

The business manager would value a system for quickly making decisions while an educator would see little value in that because it does not increase intellect. This situation is not likely to change since success in the field of education depends largely on reputation, which could be easily damaged by supporting unpopular ideas like having schools teach the use of intuition in decision-making.

The fear of a damaged reputation may also prevent some of us from embracing intuition as a valid decision-making tool. You can be at a party and mention how much success you have had with intuition and have some loud mouth try to make you sound like a fool for believing in something that statistics have shown does not work. There are statistics to back up almost any point of view. Don't be influenced by conclusions drawn from statistics; they are often erroneous. Consider the fairly well known statistic that red cars get more speeding tickets that any other color car. The assumption from this statistic is that red cars gets more tickets because they stand out more. This may be totally incorrect. Most informed people know that red paint fades three times faster than any other color. Also, red is difficult to notice in the evening which is why new fire engines are painted chartreuse. Therefore, there is likely to be a higher than average number of poorly informed people who buy red cars. This is the type of person who is less likely to be aware that they should slow down at freeway entrances and exits because that's where the highway patrol often watches for speeders, so they are liable to get more tickets. Finally, red cars tend to appeal to more flamboyant personalities. These are just the kind of people who speed. So you see that the statistic may suggest a certain conclusion, but without complete information, the conclusion can be wrong. As Mark Twain said, "figures don't lie, but liars figure".

When people are trying to influence your opinion, carefully consider what their motivations might be. Consider that people who want to impress others with their intellect often attack other's ideas. They do this because they believe they can sound impressive by criticizing the ideas of others ideas. Although these attacking types may have tremendous knowledge, they may not possess wisdom. As a result they alienate most people. Let's call these people who repeatedly attack the ideas of other's the "Contrarians" and have a little fun with them. Although kindness is the greatest wisdom, dispensing justice is a real kick. Imagine you are at a party and you make the statement that people can tell by gut feel when the person they are talking to is no longer paying attention. (This is not exactly intuition, but it will serve quite well to make the point.) If there is a Contrarian within earshot they will come over and claim that visual cues such as eye contact are responsible for this ability. At this point a typical discussion will ensue between the Contrarian and you. As in almost all discussions each side will make points *ad nauseum*, but neither is likely to change the other's mind without bringing in an unbiased group. The Contrarian knows this and is only hoping to impress us with a volley or two of quality repartee. However, this ability to tell if people are paying attention has a unique aspect. There are many people who can tell even when the other person is not visible, such as on the telephone.

You may not have this telephone ability, but many people do. Just ask those around you at the party. You will probably find that an astounding one third can do it. This is a relatively simple way to document an apparently paranormal phenomenon and gain a small victory over your Contrarian. So, when someone says that there is no scientific proof of paranormal abilities such as intuition, just realize that he or she is a Contrarian and that such proof is really common knowledge for a third of us.

The stories you find later in the book are meant to encourage you to make intuition part of your tools and to discourage you from trying to prove its validity. The only way to find out if intuition works is to use it in your own life. Leave proof to lab rats and men in little white coats. If you find that you rely on intuition almost constantly, keep that to yourself. Intuition is *still* not an accepted method of leading one's life. Friends may express disapproval at your seemingly irresponsible method of decision-making. Disapproval can be a real problem.

Acceptance is a strong social motivator and nothing to be ashamed of. Although it is stylish to say that you don't care what people think, few people are that independent. I have known a few people who truly don't care what people think and I am often glad to leave their company. Reluctance to embrace controversial concepts may be based on misguided concern for your own acceptance. Remember, a person can have downright outlandish ideas and still be very well-liked.

The things most likely to make a person well liked are that they:

♦ Don't try to impress others
♦ Avoid being critical
♦ Talk little
♦ Listen with interest, and acknowledge points that are well made.
♦ Are sensitive and kind
♦ Express their appreciation when someone does something nice for them

You will notice that these traits do not have much to do with how outlandish a person's beliefs are. You can have outlandish beliefs and still be well liked especially if you respect other's beliefs. You can show respect for the belief's of others by saying that you see how this or that could be true. This doesn't mean you agree, but telling a person about a different point-of-view, devalues their belief. Do you really need to do that?

Other Opponents

There are some other, more basic, reasons for rejecting intuition than the showmanship of the Contrarians. Some people are just plain lazy, uninterested in increasing their personal power if it requires change or effort. For these people, rejecting the validity of intuition prevents them from facing their own shortcomings. They may claim that any successful intuitive decision is the result of self-fulfilling prophecy. They would argue that, when you use intuition to make a decision, you deceptively perform the tasks that are needed to make things turn out right. Or, they may argue that the "intuitive" decision is actually based on subconscious knowledge and that nothing extraordinary is really going on. Fine. If the tools in this book increase your ability to make successful decisions and make things turn out right, call it anything you want. The important thing is whether or not it works, not the name you give it. When you succeed with these tools, *you* will not care what they are called.

If you follow the guidelines in this book and have even a little natural ability, you will be able to do amazing things. However, be cautious about telling others of your new abilities. Even good friends can be unwitting opponents. When you tell others, you start to get your ego involved (fear of failure) and thereby threaten the clarity of your intuition. It is courageous to try to convince people of an extraordinary idea, but what are your motives? If you really want to help them, find a way to put them on the road towards intuition, but avoid the temptation to prove your intuitive abilities. Use it, don't prove it. Spend time practicing and refining your intuitive tools and use it privately.

If your friends ask you about this book, just tell them that it is supposed to improve your decision-making ability and help you think of clever remarks to say during a conversation instead of five minutes after. These things are easy to believe and they will not get you into a "prove it" discussion. If your friends want to know more about intuition, encourage them to invest the time to read and follow this structured approach. It will allow them to accept intuition through a gradual and logical development. If you wish to make this book seem more interesting, tell them that it teaches you how to obtain a state of mind where problems just bounce off and away from you and what is left is peace of mind.

3 – Is This You?

If you want to develop peace of mind to help you gain access to your intuition, learn as much as you can about yourself. Learn the good as well as the bad. This is a rewarding venture, but examining yourself is tricky. The problem comes from the fact that *the easiest person to fool is yourself.* When you develop an opinion about yourself, who is there to cross-examine this opinion? Usually no one, but cross-examination is necessary. As you examine the behaviors described in this chapter, ask yourself if they describe you. It may be difficult to avoid fooling yourself into believing all the good qualities are yours and all the bad qualities belong to "those other" people. To help with this problem find a friend who knows you well and is willing to help you with this all important aspect of obtaining the peace of mind that helps so much in accessing your intuition: being able to see yourself for who you are.

Happiness

Striving for happiness sounds, on the surface, to be a good idea. Unfortunately, happiness can be misleading. Doing the happy thing, like going to the party instead of taking care of an important problem, will usually result in more problems. Although you may have a happy time at the party, peace of mind will not be the eventual result. Happiness and peace of mind may seem very similar, but they are significantly different. You can feel happy if you have distracted yourself from your troubles, but this is false happiness. Peace of mind is yours when you can contemplate your deepest feelings and be at peace.

When I was younger I sought happiness in diversion. Wine, women, and music. I attacked these diversions with gusto. I became proficient on a number of musical instruments, danced to rock and roll, and drank gin till the walls came tumbling down. Or did I do the tumbling? Regardless, I partied hardy. My social life was nonstop. I went from one whirlwind affair to another. I sure hope those women don't remember me. I was a fast-moving blob of nonsubstance; I was totally out of touch with who I was and my effect on the people I came in contact with. Is this you? Ask a friend.

As long as the distractions kept coming I felt on top of the world. Sometimes things would slow down and I wouldn't feel too good. I always thought the problem was that I had let my social calendar get a little empty, but one night I learned differently. A friend of mine talked me into going to what he called a "meeting". The people at this meeting were doing some strange things. It was a kind of meditation which I explain later in this book. Unlike most meditations, this one often has a significant effect the first time it is used. The effect is a fairly common feeling, but I didn't notice it until I walked out of the meeting. That feeling was peace.

The feeling was similar to what I felt after making love, but more permanent. It lasted through the next morning. It was a profound experience; one that I never forgot, but it took years to figure out just where that peace came from. It turned out that I had been carrying around a whole car load of bad feelings: guilt for leading a selfish life, guilt for the women I had hurt, anxiety about making mistakes at work, worry about the damage to my health due to drinking. That peace was the simple joy of being alive without the bad feelings I usually carried around. My diversions made me feel good because they distracted me from feeling what was deeper inside me, but this meditation had actually taken away my bad feelings and let me feel good even when I was not distracted with wine, women, and parties.

A person can have guilt for mistreating their friends or lovers, anxiety due to many unresolved problems, and stress for ignoring their responsibilities, but still feel good on the surface. Our modern world has many diversions that make you forget your troubles. Just forgetting them can invoke a feeling of pleasure that can be misinterpreted as happiness. Some people can watch the evening news and feel good directly afterwards. This seems to indicate that the diversion itself doesn't have to be happy; it only needs to effectively distract you. The longer you are distracted, the easier it becomes to forget your uncomfortable feelings. Finding happiness by forgetting your troubles is false happiness.

Some pleasant, superficial feelings also act as diversions and thereby promote false happiness. One common example is the feeling ones gets from obtaining attention and sympathy. It can feel very good to have people show interest in you and express sympathy, although most people swear they don't want sympathy. Unfortunately, one of the easiest ways to get people to be interested is to talk about your troubles. Everybody is attracted to disasters. This becomes a double edged sword because you are creating false happiness for yourself, which can distract you from seeking peace of mind, and thus attracts more problems.

If you are a good observer of human nature you have already noticed how problems come in groups. The reason is that talking about your problems puts you in a mind set that creates more problems. If you know a few people who always talk about their problems, you can observe this phenomenon for yourself. They have problem after problem. Is this you? Ask a friend.

Sometimes, problems only stop coming when you get so sick of them that you stop dwelling on them. There is a Christian practice called "giving it up to God." This practice is effectively the same as not dwelling, talking, or thinking about your problems. Regardless of how it works, it is an effective approach. This effectiveness supports the idea that talking or dwelling on your problems attracts more of the same.

Without a good idea of what makes you really happy, you are more likely to fall victim to false happiness. With all the effective distraction around us it may be difficult to realize that you are such a victim. This is one reason why meditation can be so important; it can help you see yourself more clearly. Unfortunately meditation takes time. Perhaps you don't have time for any more activities, but maybe one of your distractions takes up more time than you realize. Perhaps you have a powerful distraction that overcomes your deeper feelings *and* your motivation to do anything. Do you have such a distraction in your life?.

The Blue Haze

Or Strange Idea #2

The Blue Haze is a poem written by Dixie Pine. The poem tells a scary story that seems at first like an alien invasion. The blue haze peacefully spreads from one house to the next, quietly subduing the inhabitants. By the end of the poem, it is evening and looking over the country side, you can see a glowing blue haze in the living rooms of every house. The occupant's minds slowly progressing towards stagnation, their lives towards emptiness. The blue haze is the blue light that a TV creates in a dark room.

The emptiness that comes from an unfulfilling life can motivate you to either add real value to your life or escape from it. The more you escape from your life, the less you put into it and, usually, the worse it gets. If this happens, the only time you can feel good may be when you are distracted. There is an entire world waiting and willing to perform this distraction for you. Just push a button and this world is yours. The sensationalism that you see when you turn on your TV is the main ingredient of this world. With such an effective and easy to use distractor, a person is easily swept away. When people in this situation try to use their intuition, it will be inaccessible because the sensationalism of TV has desensitized them to their own feelings. To access deeper feelings, most people need to increase their sensitivity not reduce it.

For many years I didn't have a TV. This changed when I was recovering from an operation. I read so much that I started getting concerned for my eyes. In self-defense, I finally purchased a TV to help occupy many weeks of inactivity. After reading good books for years, it was shocking to find that so many shows on TV were poorly written. Ninety percent of the shows had plots that depicted an epic struggle against a problem that most of us could fix in five minutes. These shows were interspersed with violent murders that should upset anyone, but I suspect that most viewers had become hardened to seeing the lives of human beings snuffed out. A worse effect on our belief of the sanctity of life I couldn't imagine. The dialogue of these shows did demonstrate how some murders were justifiable. I found myself thinking, if the writer of this show insults my intelligence once more....

Watching educational TV is a step in the right direction. However, ask someone what they learned from an hour of educational TV and they will be hard pressed to report on more than a minute's worth of information. Then ask a person who is reading a nonfiction book to tell you a little about it. They will have tons of information. Educational TV is a more wholesome distraction because somebody is usually not being killed every five minutes (war documentaries excluded). However, watching TV in any form is too passive an activity to stimulate our thinking processes the way reading or working can. Often, as you watch TV, you stop thinking. You give up your imagination and enter a trance-like state where there is little brain activity. With a book, *you* actively create pictures from the words or develop tangents which *you* can easily follow without missing any part of the book by simply putting it down for a minute or two.

TV gets to the lower, more animal instincts like fear, hate, and revenge very effectively. In this way TV can keep you emotionally stimulated but intellectually passive for hours. What you receive for your invested time is the dulling of your higher mental functions. To add insult to injury, you are forced to watch endless commercials, which often seem to be directed at people with IQ's below 80. Is this you? How many hours a day do you watch the box?

Many people expose themselves to TV news with the belief that they are being informed. It is not the media's aim to inform you. Their aim is to capture the biggest audience and thereby make the most money. Some people conclude that they can be adequately informed by TV news because most of the facts reported are true. Though the facts *may* be true, the overall picture they present can be very misleading.

For nearly four years I worked on F-15s. I spent countless hours with pilots reviewing its performance in training missions, helping flightline troops troubleshoot their more difficult problems, and tracking spare parts problems. I had an overall picture of the worth of that jet that few people even in the Air Force were privy to. I had also worked on other jet fighters to form a good comparison. So I was very interested when a news show was going to dedicate 15 minutes to this jet.

50

I went to a friend's house to watch the show. I was entertained throughout. However, when the segment was over I was amazed. Almost every fact that was reported about the F-15 was correct, but the overall impression of the performance and maintainability of the aircraft was the complete opposite of what I knew to be true. This was possible because the producers only selected the most sensational facts to present.

Another problem with TV news is the proliferation of depressing and totally unnewsworthy subjects like individual murder cases and their grisly details. True, it is important to know the overall effect of your local law enforcement, however, exposing yourself to the atrocities of deranged people is unsettling to your deeper feelings. It also promotes fear which is the most common block to your intuition. Unlike newspapers or magazines, it is difficult to skip over these horrible stories on TV news. Do you let dread creep into your life on a regular, 6 o'clock news schedule?

The significant events in today's world are quite complicated, making it difficult for anyone to possess a sufficient amount of information upon which to base a valid opinion. This is especially true if you get your information primarily from TV news. If an issue is important to you, avoid TV news and read as much as you can on the subject in books. Books are more carefully researched than newspaper stories.

Information concerning the actions of our governmental representatives is important to all of us and necessary for responsible political activity such as voting, letter writing, etc. Unfortunately, such information is not exciting enough to get into TV news. There is, however, reliable information available, such as newsletters and online services. Finding these sources will allow you to become informed sufficiently to vote responsibly and avoid the manipulative sensationalism of TV news. Although I avoid TV and newspapers, I accurately predicted the fall of Russian communism two years before Gorbachev started his massive reforms by selective reading. Avoid the bad feeling of TV news. Control what information you ingest; read books or in-depth reports. Don't worry, during conversations on current events that you haven't investigated, there is no need to feel inadequate because you can't contribute. You can do something better: make someone feel good by asking for their opinions. This is what "the informed" are hoping you will do so they will have the opportunity to sound intelligent. You will gain their warmest regard.

After avoiding TV news for many years, I am always shocked by how strongly it affects me when I do occasionally see some. The subject on the news is usually one of the following: revolting violence, depressing economics, or infuriating governmental incompetence, each of which makes me feel over-stimulated, distracted, and upset. This inner discomfort will make you want to move away from your self-awareness, which is exactly the opposite of what you need to do to access your intuition. Furthermore, a person who submits to any kind of TV on a regular basis is likely to generate guilt over a conscious or unconscious recognition that they have been wasting valuable hours of their life. Guilt is one of those low level feelings that interferes with accessing your intuition.

Another disturbing element of TV is the over simplified road to happiness that typifies many TV story endings. These "modern myths" promise that all you need to do is obtain them and you will be happy. Although TV is a major producer of these myths, there are many other sources. You may want to look at a few modern myths and see if you believe in any.

Modern Myths

Or Strange Ideas #3 to #7

Our modern world is full of many myths that promise happiness. They are wonderful in appearance, but lacking in substance. Everyday you are bombarded with advertisements carefully designed to convince you that you need this or that product. Through this constant bombardment, you are lead to believe the myth that possessions can make you happy. As far as happiness is concerned, possessions are only distractions, and like all distractions they are temporary. If you know yourself well, you will realize how few possessions you really need to be happy. The most valuable asset in your search for peace of mind and happiness is good character, not good possessions. The old bumper sticker "Whoever dies with the most toys wins" may be true, but you win

52

the boobe prize. The peace of mind that allows easy access to your intuition is not achieved by buying fancy cars and expensive toys, it is achieved with elements of your character which allow you to be caring, diligent, and self-aware. Until you develop a sense of value which cherishes these and other attributes, the modern myths, like possessions, will be hard to resist.

The Rich Myth

Many people think riches bring happiness. Of course if you are too poor to keep a roof over your head it is very hard to be happy. However, if you have enough money to do most anything you want, it can be just as hard to be really happy. People with endless amounts of money can keep themselves distracted most of the time and rarely get in touch with their need to create, contribute, and improve. If their distractions stop, even for a short time, they are likely to feel very bad. They will never feel the deep satisfaction that comes with real happiness unless they stop distracting themselves and start the often unpleasant task of getting to know themselves. What have you done that taught you a lot about yourself? Would it have happened if you were very rich? Can you do something similar again?

The Lovers Myth

If you believe that finding a lover is all you need to become happy, then you are believing in the lovers myth. You must be able to find happiness without an intimate relationship before you have any real chance of finding happiness in one. If you choose a partner to fill a gap in your life you will go from one unsatisfying relationship to another. Is this you?

A relationship should enrich your life. The gap filling approach is a good example of looking outside of yourself when you need to be looking inside yourself. When you succeed in creating a person within yourself that you can love, only then will you attract a person on the outside that can love you even after you have let down your walls. Learn to respect and love yourself and the right person will be attracted to you.

In the mean time, where is happiness to be found? The answer is: with your friends. Often the people who expect the least from us are the people who will end up giving us the most pleasure. Doing a small, unexpected kindness for a friend will get a warm reaction as it would in an intimate relationship. However, such kindness are expected and often required in intimate relationships. These and other expectations brought on by the myth place intimate relationships on an emotional roller coaster ride. In comparison, friendships are often healthier, more rewarding and long lasting. Some ideas on making and maintaining friendships can be found in the section Making Good Friends in chapter 4, Obtaining Peace of Mind.

The Marriage Myth

If you believe that marriage will help your relationship stay healthy, then you believe in the marriage myth. Marriage will tend to keep you physically together; it will not keep you happy or your relationship healthy. It is amazing that people say congratulations when they hear of a person's marriage. It is most likely that the couple is embarking on a road that will ruin the romance that they currently hold so dear. The result might even be the most devastating emotional experience that people face: divorce.

Surely, a union that starts out with a big lie, told in front of so many people, is likely to end badly. What lie? The promise to love each other for the rest of your lives is the big lie. Love is an emotion. You can't control your love for one week, never mind the rest of your live; that's why it's called an emotion. Regardless of the good intentions, a promise to control something that you can't control is a lie. On the other hand some people stay together despite the loss of the love that originally brought them together. People like Melissa and Mark. They may claim to love each other, but aside from occasional sex, there is no display of affection and no kindness. One year Melissa accompanied Mark to one of his yearly checkups. After the checkup the doctor took the Melissa aside and told her, "Your husband has a very serious condition. If you don't follow these directions, your husband will surely die:

1. Each morning, fix him a healthy breakfast and send him off to work in a good mood.

2. At lunch, make him a warm nutritious meal and put him in a good frame of mind before he goes back to work.
3. For dinner, fix an especially nice meal and don't burden him with household chores.
4. Have sex with him several times a week and make sure that he is happy.

On the way home, Mark asked Melissa what the doctor said. She replied, "You're going to die."

Staying together even though the relationship has died is a terrible way to live, but many people do just that. Living in the resulting environment of denial and devaluation can easily prevent contact with intuition. Although most marriages are beyond repair a good marriage is not impossible. Enlightened awareness, chemistry, and respect are always needed. A commitment to stay together is not.

An often over-looked and essential aspect of all relationships is respect. When a person close to you is inconsiderate, you start to lose respect for them. You feel that they are putting their personal desires ahead of their concern for you and the relationship. It is a common observation that marriage doesn't work any more because people are not truly committed to each other. That observation may have missed the real cause. No matter how committed you are to each other, your relationship will die if you lose respect. Your commitment will then help keep you in a bad relationship. What good is that? The marriage myth, with its expectation of relationship longevity, has many pitfalls such as creating a false feeling of security. The carelessness that comes with this false security can easily lead to a loss of respect. Has this happened to you?

The Child Myth

Sometimes when a marriage just isn't fulfilling, it feels like something is missing. This can be misinterpreted as a reason to have children. The decision to take on a 20 year project that you can't walk away from is too important to leave to chance. If your relationship isn't strong it will not survive the strain of parenting. Although there are potentially wonderful joys involved with creating a responsible, contributing adult, you must look at or experience (even better) the actions you must take to achieve your goals. Thankfully, you can have near-to-real-life family experiences before committing to a 20 year long project. Follow the twelve simple steps below and see how fulfilling they are.

1. Women: to prepare for maternity, put on a dressing gown and stick a beanbag down the front. Leave it there for 9 months. After 9 months, take out 10% of the beans. Men: to prepare for paternity, go to the local chemist, tip the contents of your wallet on the counter, and tell the pharmacist to help himself. Then go to the supermarket. Arrange to have your salary paid directly to their head office. Go home. Pick up the paper. Read it for the last time.

2. Find a couple who are already parents and berate them about their methods of discipline, lack of patience, appallingly low tolerance levels, and how they have allowed their children to run riot. Suggest ways in which they might improve their child's sleeping habits, toilet training, table manners and overall behavior. Enjoy it for it'll probably be the last time in your life that you have any clue about child rearing.

3. To discover how the nights will feel, walk around the living room from 5pm to 10pm carrying a bag of water weighing approximately 12 lb. At 10pm put the bag down, set the alarm for midnight, and go to sleep. Get up at 12am and walk around the living room again, with the bag, until 1am. Put the alarm on for 3am. As you can't get back to sleep get up at 2am and make a drink. Go to bed at 2:45am. Get up again at 3am when the alarm goes off. Sing songs in the dark until 4am. Put the alarm on for 5am. Get up. Make breakfast. Keep this up for 5 years. Look cheerful.

4. Can you stand the mess children make? To find out, first smear marmalade onto the sofa and jam onto the curtains. Hide a fish finger behind the stereo and leave it there all summer. Stick your fingers in the flower beds then rub them on the clean walls. Cover the stains with crayons. How does that look?

5. Dressing small children is not as easy as it seems: first buy an octopus and a string bag. Attempt to put the octopus into the string

56

bag so that none of the arms hang out. Time allowed for this: all morning.

6. Take an egg carton. Using a pair of scissors and a pot of paint, turn it into an alligator. Now take a toilet tube. Using only tape and a piece of foil, turn it into a Christmas tree decoration. Last, take a milk container, a ping pong ball, and an empty box of Coco Puffs and make an exact replica of the Eiffel Tower. Congratulations. You have just qualified for a place on the playground committee.

7. Forget the Peugeot 205 and buy a Sierra. And don't think you can leave it out in the driveway spotless and shining. Family cars don't look like that. Buy a chocolate ice-cream cone and put it in the glove compartment. Leave it there. Get a grease gun. Shoot some in the cassette player. Take three peeled bananas. Mash them down the back seats. Run a garden rake along both sides of the car. There. Perfect.

8. Get ready to go out. Wait outside the bathroom for half an hour. Go out the front door. Come in again. Go out. Come back in. Go out again. Walk down the front path. Walk back up it. Walk down it again. Walk very slowly down the road for 5 minutes. Stop to inspect minutely every cigarette end, piece of used chewing gum, dirty tissue and dead insect along the way. Retrace your steps. Scream that you've had as much as you can stand, until the neighbors come out and stare at you. Give up and go back into the house. You are now just about ready to take a small child for a walk.

9. Always repeat everything you say at least five times.

10. Go to your local supermarket. Take with you the nearest thing you can find to a pre-school child a fully grown goat is excellent. If you intend to have more than one child, take more than one goat. Buy your week's groceries without letting the goats out of your sight. Pay for everything the goats eat or destroy.

11. Hollow out a melon. Make a small hole in the side. Suspend it from the ceiling and swing it from side to side. Now get a bowl of soggy corn flakes and attempt to spoon it into the swaying melon by pretending to be an airplane. Continue until half the corn flakes is gone. Tip the rest into your lap, making sure that a lot of it falls on the floor. You are now ready to feed a 12 month old baby.

12. Realize that after having children, nothing in the first eleven simple steps above will ever again hold any humor for you. They will be you.

If you believe in reincarnation, realize that the values and character developed by child rearing is probably common to most of your other lifetimes. You are now in a unique period of history where there is free time to experience many things other than family and work. Instead of creating a need to fulfill (such as having a helpless child), consider enriching your life with a wide range of experiences. Don't fall for the child myth; consider developing a life that has the freedom to explore any interest and pursue any dream.

Problem Myth
It can be difficult to avoid the traps. Television creates beautiful, rich, and important appearing characters who have everything you want. It is normal to envy them. Unfortunately, their behavior is perverted for the benefit of the plot. Their decisions are designed to increase the drama of the show. This means that they make decisions that create more problems. In this way you are subtly conditioned to react to problems in such a way as to create more problems. Subconsciously, you learn that having problems makes you appear important. Appearing important will get you attention and impress others. On the other hand, being happy can make you appear unimportant because you don't have a dramatic life. TV stories need problems to make them dramatic, but such a life style pushes people further from their intuition. If you are unaware of this, you can get sucked into the unconscious "I gotta have problems to be important" trap. Ever been so trapped?

Your Body May Motivate You
Ask any doctor how intelligent he or she believes our bodies are and you may be surprised at the awe that most doctors have of the body. Ask an one who works with energy flow, such as an acupuncturist, what they thing of our bodies and you may learn your body can become ill in order to call your attention to unresolved issues. In response to unresolved

issues or other emotional issues, our bodies create energy blocks that prevent the healthy flow of energy sometimes called chi. This causes illness. The type of illness caused by unresolved issues often has one or two distinct characteristics. It can be difficult to diagnose, and/or it often responds to treatments, but soon recurs. If you know someone who has an ailment that fits this description, encourage them to find a way to face themselves. It may take therapy, long talks with a friend, or writing in a journal, but they must get help. It is too easy to fool yourself.

A friend of mine started to have knee pain about eight years ago. At first it was so severe that she wasn't able to walk. After a few days in the hospital, she was able to walk for short periods, but then the pain would return. Although the pain had decreased a bit, it zapped her energy and made it almost impossible for her to work. She went to many medical doctors and specialists, but the solution evaded her. She eventually had an operation on one knee. They found nothing wrong. Although the surgery was exploratory it took a year for her to fully recover.

My friend went from one treatment to another. She tried chiropractors, neurosurgeons, physical therapists, drugs, and vitamins. She even tried cod liver oil. Many of the treatments had good results, but they never worked long. The pain affected her life so much that she quit work to concentrate on getting better. She started taking classes in anatomy and physiology, partly to help her understand what was wrong and partly to develop a new career that would create less stress. She learned a lot but found no relief. Soon she was using a wheelchair when she went places that required walking or standing for a sustained period.

Finally, she went to a holistic doctor who used western medicine, acupuncture, and a bit of psychology. After a few long talks and examinations, the doctor's opinion was that she simply lacked an emotional release. The doctor then discovered something significant about her childhood. She was prohibited from making noise when she was young. The house had to be quiet because her mother taught piano. My friend, who was a naturally boisterous child, was denied her natural form of release. She had no outlet for her childhood frustrations and anguishes and she carried this conditioning into adulthood.

After seeing the holistic doctor she started changing her ways. Now, she no longer suppresses her feelings, but lets them out. Through sickness, her body forced her to face herself and eventually find peace of mind. The wheelchair has two flat tires and some cobwebs. It never looked better.

It seems that the medical profession is giving more credibility these days to the relationship between emotional issues and health problems. Holistic medicine is one of the results, and its growth may be one measure of modern man's self-awareness. All illnesses may not be caused by emotional problems. Sometimes things just break down. However, there may also be a higher reason. Perhaps there must be sickness in order to challenge our healing skills and increase our knowledge.

Once you have started on the road to peace of mind, you may discover that it affects your health. Peace of mind helps you remain free of "blocks." Blocks are generally caused by emotions. Unresolved emotional issues not only interfere with intuition, but can cause health problems. Acupuncture, like a number of other healing techniques, recognizes that these emotional issues can cause obstructions to the natural flow of energy through our bodies and thus cause health problems. In acupuncture, as well as in other new age health disciplines, these obstructions are called blocks. The term block fits well with intuition considerations and will be used from now on to refer to emotional residue as well as the stronger, more observable feelings that might interfere with your intuition. For example, there is a common practice that creates blocks very effectively. This practice relates to your response to pressure. The practice is called stress.

Stress

Stress is insidious. The blocks that it causes continue even after the stress is gone. Even if you remove blocks daily, new stress will generate new blocks. Blocks caused by stress are among the most health destructive blocks and will prevent you from achieving peace of mind.

I used to think that I kept my stress at a low level because people at work were always asking me how I stayed so calm. Then, I spent a four day weekend at a lake with no plans except to rent a canoe with my friend and let it drift. After the third day I noticed that I was very "cleaned out" (few if any blocks to remove) when I meditated. My last night at the lake I dreamed about flying. (Flying dreams are indicative of feeling carefree.) I returned home and the next day started back to work. The night after my first day at work I dreamed that I was drowning someone in a swimming pool. Apparently my work was affecting my peace of mind even though I appeared calm. I resolved to adopt the point of view and ideas written below. It worked.

Consider this: your job does not give you stress. Unavoidable pressure can be produced by your job, but you choose how you respond to it. You make the unconscious decision that the situation requires you to be stressed. It can be very difficult, but you can make a conscious decision to respond differently. Making this conscious decision may be easier if you can take an honest look at possible reasons why your response to pressure is stress. Some people give themselves stress to appear important, to get attention or to get their own way in the work place. At home the stressed out spouse may get sympathy and reduced responsibilities. If this is you, do you think you could hide that fact from yourself?

There is another practice that creates blocks very effectively. It is even more destructive than stress. One of the worst things about this practice is that it is often viewed as an act of kindness. I call this practice negative visualizations. You call it something else and probably do it every week.

Negative Visualizations/Creating Disasters

Or Strange Idea #8

In recent years, positive visualization has received increased acceptance as witnessed by the popularity of such books as Shakti Gawain's *Creative Visualizations*, which has sold over a million copies. More and more people are discovering that they can affect the outcome of events by visualizing the desired goal or by visualizing the processes that are needed to achieve that goal. This idea has spread from bumper stickers saying, "Visualize Peace" to champion athletes who visualize making the basket or scoring the goal.

If positive visualizations work, what about negative visualizations? What about visualizing the worst outcome? Would that increase the probability of failure? The answer is yes; negative visualizations increase the probability of failure and they are even more effective than positive visualizations.

It seems that the more attention and emotion a person puts into a visualization, the more vivid it becomes and the better it works. Therefore, negative visualizations would work better than positive visualizations due to the fact that problems and disasters almost always get more attention and generate more emotion than positive occurrences. Visualizing some disasters can even invoke fear, one of our strongest emotions, and therefore make the visualization that much stronger.

It is a sad fact that many of us are attracted to disasters like moths to a flame, and that some people find good news boring. This tendency can be clearly seen by observing various media that have become successful by presenting bad news and disasters. In order for a large commercial TV station or magazine to be successful they must attract a large audience. In order to do this they must broadcast subjects that attract people and keep their attention. Take a look at newspapers and TV. Compare the number of stories about happy events to the stories about problems, disasters, and violence. What are people most attracted to? What gets their maximum attention and their strongest emotional involvement? Do you drift towards the disasters, the negativity?

It looks like we have found a new and powerful tool if we are interested in accomplishing negative things. On the other hand, perhaps this is actually an old tool with a new name. Perhaps negative visualization is really worry. Can you see any significant difference?

How to Focus on the Positive

Or Strange Idea #9

The following tool is the easiest way to bring positive events into your life. I try to do it every day. The people I have convinced to do it have reported amazing results, their lives were turned around and they think I am a guru. But this is really too simple. Here is the procedure:

1. Everyday, preferably in the morning, write down the good things that happened the day before. They do not have to be important things,

they could be how pleasant the air felt when you came out of work for lunch or getting past a long traffic light before it turned red.

That's it, one step.

Although this sounds easy, you may have difficulty remembering positive things. You may have to *develop a habit of remembering positive things.* Negative events are much more easy to remember because:

◆ Negative things have more emotional impact.
◆ Relating negative occurrences to friends or loved ones gets more attention and evokes more love from them.

Therefore, we hold onto negative memories more closely than positive memories. The important question to ask yourself: is there a price to pay for having negative events closer to the forefront of our minds? I have proven to myself over and over again that there is most certainty a price to pay. When I get out of the habit of writing down the good things from the day before, bad things start happening. What usually happens next is that I ask myself, why are all these bad things happening? The answer is almost always, "you haven't been writing down the good things."

The most telling aspect of my positive event writing is what recently happened the first day I went back to my writing habit. At first, I couldn't think of a single positive thing that happened the day before. I was convinced that not one positive thing had happened. I sat there looking at a blank page and started to relax and let my mind wonder. After a couple of minutes, I finally started to remember good things from the day before. I remember many more good things than I usually did and these were big things. It turned out that the day before had been a terrific day, but I had not been able to remember anything positive. Now that I am back in the habit, I can even remember little things that happened. I am living in the positive world again.

Self Responsibility

If a person accepts responsibility for the trouble he or she, innocently or inadvertently caused, the control they have over their life increases. Rationalizations are easy to think up, but reduce our acknowledgement of our control over our reality. Pretty soon, we believe that we don't have control. That is not true.

In childhood, some people learn to avoid punishment by searching for excuses or, even better, someone else to blame. This attitude can continue into their adult lives where their increased rationalizing abilities will make them impossible to get along with. They will blame their difficulties on everything or everybody but themselves. Their problems will repeat again and again because they never recognize what *they do* that causes the problem. They will be constantly tormented by problems, never achieve peace of mind, and never realize control over their life. Is this you? If it is, you wouldn't admit it would you?

Self responsibility means looking for your action or *attitude* (no matter how insignificant) that could have caused the problem. Never mind who had more control over the situation or who contributed what to cause the problem. The other person's level of responsibility is unimportant. That's their problem. What matters is your part, no matter how big or small; it could have made the difference. When you find out where your responsibility lies (even if it was just a bad attitude), then you can do something positive to prevent such problems. You are then improving yourself. Looking for a justification or defending your mistakes is the opposite of self responsibility. It accomplishes nothing for you and makes people feel annoyed.

People who think that they can improve their image by explaining why they are not responsible are missing a number of points:

1. People usually form their opinion of a person shortly after being introduced.
2. If people already like you, they will find "explanations" when you make mistakes.
3. If they dislike you and you try to explain how the problem was not your fault, they will think you are weaseling out just like they knew you would.

The best thing you can do in the face of a mistake is to acknowledge your part, "you know, I could have done something that would have prevented the problem." Who ever says that? Don't we usually talk about how something was not our responsibility?

General Responsibility

Responsibility can be divided into two types. One is responsibility for something that occurred. The other is responsibility for something that needs to get done. Both can affect peace of mind. If you have so many things to get done that you cannot accomplish them, then you can never feel satisfied. You can only feel pressured. If this is the case, reducing your responsibilities will help you find peace of mind. If all of your responsibilities absolutely must be accomplished, a good loud call for help could solve your problems. Unfortunately, some people never ask for help. They don't trust others to do it right or their ego is tied up with finishing everything themselves. Such attitudes make peace of mind difficult. Is this you? Ask a friend.

It takes courage to speak out and tell people that you are unable to meet some responsibilities. It may be difficult to convince someone that they must accept some of your tasks, but these things must be done if you want to have peace of mind. If you maintain too many responsibilities and start failing to meet them, there will always be excuses, but presenting excuses and giving "explanations" will cause resentment from those around you. Your response to this resentment will result in low level feelings that can block your intuition.

So perhaps you have resolved to handle your responsibilities in a manner that will ensure peace of mind, but what if the people around you ignore their responsibility? What will you do with your resentment?.

Resentment

Or Strange Idea #10

"Sorry", the ever ready, ultra easy, one size fits all apology. Why is saying that word supposed to be enough to repair the damage or disappointment when someone is undependable, thoughtless, or even mean? It is such an easy word to say; how can it accomplish so much good? Perhaps it can't. The apparent good accomplished by saying sorry may be misleading. The actual effect in many cases is totally negative. This negative effect comes in the form of resentment. People are considered mean if they do not forgive someone who says the "S" word. For appearance's sake, and to keep the peace, many of us give in and accept the apology, even though we are unsatisfied. The resentment this breeds will prevent peace of mind until the issues that caused the resentment are resolved. Is this you? Ask a friend.

When resentment is allowed to grow, couples can become pretty destructive. Some couples seem to wait for each other to make a mistake so they can point it out. You probably know people like this. Sometimes they hide their criticism behind a joking manner. If their partner really gets upset they always fall back on, "Hey, I was just joking. Can't you take a joke?" It is surprising that people stay in such destructive relationships. When they are together, neither can have any peace of mind because resentment is always near the surface. What makes this situation most sad is that the couples that display this behavior always seem to live together. This means many hours of their lives are spent with someone who is trying to make them pay for past transgressions. Of course, the reason they always seem to live together is that people who lived separately would simply stop seeing each other when this type of treatment started. People who live together in the resentment trap must prefer the bad treatment to the pain, embarrassment, and effort of breaking up. It is easy to see how someone can fall into the resentment trap, but remaining in it demonstrates a distorted sense of value and ultimately leads to suppressed feelings that block access to one's intuition.

There are a number of ways that resentment can develop in a relationship besides over-use of the S word. Here are just two:

1. When one person thinks that they are giving more than the other.
2. When one person thinks the other is being too critical.

Once resentment gets a foothold, it is hard to recover. Have you ever been like this?

Anger

Anger has a strong effect on many aspects of our lives. Anger in personal interactions is disturbing, distressing, destructive, and disruptive, just to name the D's. Anger manufactures so many disquieting feelings that it distances a person from their deeper feelings, where their intuition resides. Using anger regularly can completely prevent contact with intuition. Many situations can cause anger. Fear can cause anger. One interesting fear is the fear of being caught. Some transgressions such as dishonesty or prejudice can produce strong fear of being caught. In these situations, we can dread being caught so strongly that we stop thinking and start acting in a primitive manner.

Think back to an incident when you were young and were caught doing something that was very wrong. Perhaps it was something dishonest and hurt a number of people or something valuable. Everybody makes mistakes, but often they are blessedly hard to remember. Once you remember one, picture the exact moment when you were confronted with your error. It felt terrible didn't it? Some of us learn at this early age that we can get rid of this terrible feeling very quickly. The method is simple; just find something, anything to get angry about. There is almost always something to get angry about in a pinch. Even if it doesn't make a lot of sense, the anger will make the terrible feeling go away. Usually the accused can turn the situation to their advantage by claiming that the accuser is being overly critical, unfair, hypersensitive, always nagging... the defenses are endless. The end result is a person who has trained themselves to get angry instead of responsible because it feels better, at least initially. There is no chance of peace of mind for such a person; too many issues will be left unresolved. Have you ever used anger like this?

Anger is a very effective weapon and it has a great defense: they made me angry, therefore, "they" are in the wrong. People learn early that getting angry works. Anger will get them the floor in most any meeting. In discussions, anger can make an opponent yield because he or she wants to avoid confrontation. Subtly controlled anger allows people to verbally brutalize others while making themselves appear to be responsible for annoying you. A person could operate like this for years and always feel right. Then, one day they realize that they have alienated everyone they know.

A person can use anger to blame others or they can follow the words of a wise old man, my swimming coach. I remember this one bit of wisdom above all else because whenever I have applied it, things turn out so well for me. He said, "A wise man always assumes half the responsibility." This simple wisdom has allowed me to fix disastrous misunderstandings involving some very difficult people.

When you come in close contact with your deeper feelings, you may become aware of the strength and surprising longevity of the negative feelings that anger creates. If you decide to stop using anger, you may have to confront a number of fears. It is distressing, even terrifying, to accept responsibility for mistakes and disasters. It can take great courage, but a habit of using anger can erode your courage. You may have to learn how to confront fear all over. This can be difficult, but it may be necessary if you want to reliably access your intuition.

Fear

Or Strange Idea #11

Some people are afraid of things that can occur in everyday life. If such a person wants to reliably access their intuition they must avoid these things or overcome the fear they create. Do you have fears about things that can happen in everyday life?

One early spring day about 15 years ago when I was living in Germany, I went with a friend to visit a farmer. The farmer offered to let me ride one of his horses. He said that the horse had been in the barn all winter, but since I was from the wild west I should be able to handle him. I know how wild a horse can get when they have been cooped up for a long time (like a German winter), but I thought I would just hang on until he wore himself out. I started to get a little nervous when the farmer put a bridle on the horse without a bit. I knew that without one I wouldn't have much control.

Once I mounted, I decided to let the horse start when he was good and ready. At first he didn't move, but when he realized that he had his freedom he did a perfect imitation of a guided missile. The acceleration caught me off guard and I almost fell over backwards. By the time I got forward he had started a right turn around the corner of the main barn. I leaned into the turn and stayed on with no problem. The next turn was very soon and to the left. I straightened up and started leaning to the left when suddenly the horse turned to the right, toward a small foot path I hadn't seen before. I tried to stay on with all my strength, but it was very hard. There I was hanging way out on the left side of the horse while he was making an unbelievably tight right turn.

I felt like I was pulling 5 G's with my right thigh taking all the force. The fall was inevitable. I suddenly realized that if I fought it much longer I would be landing on a barbed wire fence. It was time to let that beast go his own way. As I headed back to mother earth, I rotated in the air so I could use my feet to stop me from going into the fence. I came to a stop flat on my back with the bottom of both boots tight against the lowest wire of the fence. Once again, being a gymnast had saved my posterior. I was pretty shaken. Things happened so fast, I didn't know what scared me more; the speed of the take off, the height of the fall, or the barbed wire. All the farmer saw was a horse and rider disappear behind the main barn at a great rate and only a horse emerge, victoriously, on the other side.

I understand the theory of getting right back up on the horse that throws you. If you don't, you may be afraid of horses forever. I had every intention of getting back on that guided missile, but I was hurt. I landed on the ground fine, but I had pulled a muscle in my right thigh when I was struggling to stay on the horse. There was no way I could ride. I limped back to the farmer feeling like a tinhorn from Los Angeles.

Fifteen years later I was making one of my regular visits to see my friend Coleen, who raises horses. She is becoming known for the extremely friendly and loving Arabian Pintos she breeds, but I still declined her many invitations to go riding. For years I have used my bad back as an excuse. The truth is that I was still afraid of horses because of that fall so long ago. What's worse, her horses know it.

From time to time, I lend Coleen a hand fixing fences. The problem is that as soon as her horses smell me in the pasture they think, "hey, here comes the pushover; let's have some fun". They stroll over like the grass is the best right by me, then act surprised to see somebody standing there. Soon they start pushing me around with their heads. These animals are big. And look at those hoofs. The fear is making my stomach queasy. Coleen tells me I should stand up to them. I yell, "Hey!" at them, but they know I'm scared and they just keep pushing me around until Coleen comes over and quietly says, "Hey." Then, they stop in their tracks and I search around for my ego.

Fear may be costing you more than your realize. Whenever your fears are turned on, you create a big block that can interfere with accessing your intuition. Often the people who avoid confronting their fear avoid confronting many issues. Learning how to confront your fears can teach you to confront your issues. Is fear preventing you from becoming all you can be? Do your fears make you look bad? Is this you? Ask a friend.

4 – *Obtaining Peace of Mind*

If you are stressed, consumed by worry, or oppressed by emotional baggage, accessing your intuition may be impossible. If you have peace of mind, accessing your intuition becomes a simple procedure. However, there is no simple one-size-fits-all road to peace of mind; each person's road to peace of mind is personal and unique. Also, the generally believed notions of what is necessary to be happy or obtain peace of mind are usually false. Men with great wealth become consumed with making more and more money because they cannot accept the fact that money – the thing they have valued so greatly all their life – cannot bring them lasting happiness. Following the concepts in this book does not guarantee that you will find your unique road to peace of mind, but it will help you eliminate a few false ones.

Anger that persists, wrongs you have not atoned for, unresolved relationship problems, unmet responsibilities; all these and more result in blocks that can remain for a long time. Learning to remove these blocks is a major step toward peace of mind. Maintaining peace of mind for the majority of your waking hours usually requires the kind of work that increases self-awareness. This type of work can be painful, but any progress is a worthy accomplishment. Not only does this type of progress aid your access to your intuition, it also improves your mental and physical health.

Sometimes, as you strive to bring peace into your life, a few issues may arise. Sometimes they require your attention or peace seems impossible. You can decide to work the issue or continue to ignore it. It is not as hard to ignore things as one might think because of the following little known fact:

The easiest person in the world to fool is yourself.

Who Has Peace of Mind?

There are two types of people who *appear* to have peace of mind. The first are people who have high personal integrity, remain calm in tense situations, don't worry, are dependable, take care of their business, and resolve their personal issues. They are free of disturbing feelings because they meet their responsibilities, treat others with consideration, and accomplish things that allow them to feel good about themselves. This first group is fairly rare and they often lead simple lives that might preclude them from making many acquaintances. You might, however, know one or two.

The second type of person that appears to have peace of mind is not of much use to us as an example. However, they are interesting in their own right. These folks achieve their freedom by truly not caring. No matter how badly they disappoint people or shirk their responsibilities, they feel no remorse. You might call this kind of person totally unscrupulous. These people are even rarer than those in the first group. If you are lucky, you do not currently know any. However, you may have known one or two when you were younger. As you have grown older, you have most likely disassociated yourself from people like this. Also people with this personality tend to disappear from our lives at an earlier age. They die young, end up in prison, or pursue a career in politics. Do you remember any from your youth? Try to recall if they didn't have a gift for the intuitive. Interesting, isn't it? These people are often in touch with their intuition because they care so little about anything that they have few disturbing feelings to interfere with accessing their intuition.

No Sacrifices Required

Although we have fewer monasteries than a few centuries ago, some people still abandon the materialistic goals of modern society for more altruistic ones and head for India to seek enlightenment. If they were doing this to obtain peace of mind, the trip was unnecessary. Sacrifices are not required. The quest for peace of mind and the pursuit of material gain do not have to conflict.

The anti-materialism of the 60's gave way to the new materialism of the 80's when it became more acceptable to pursue material things, to want control over our lives, and to create goals and stress ourselves to achieve them. At the same time there has been an increased acceptance of the more extraordinary powers of the mind and spirit. Contrary to the thinking of the 60's, these two concepts can actually work together. Properly managed, they can produce a balance between awareness and security that is essential to achieving peace of mind. With a good balance of ambition and self-awareness you can create a life full of people and things to love. However, as your self-awareness increases, your values may change. For example, when you look for a new job, you may realize that the quality of people you work with is more important than career advancement.

As you make decisions on your road towards awareness and security, you may have a new and valuable tool. Instead of analyzing questionable facts to make a decision, you may learn to feel the best decision. Such a valuable tool will accelerate your progress towards awareness and security.

Preventing Peace of Mind

Or Strange Ideas #12 to #21
The intricacies of society have changed drastically in recent years but our education rarely prepares us for these changes. To obtain peace of mind in today's world a person must develop awareness and abilities to deal with issues like:

Self Responsibility	Anger
Fear	Annoyance
Resentment	Problem solving
Motivation	Dependability
Stress	Friendship

These issues relate closely to obtaining peace of mind and intuition. By having addressed these issues successfully, a person develops the confidence needed for peace of mind. There are many different roads that lead towards increased peace of mind. The best road is the one you find yourself. To find your road, look at your current situation and examine your goals. Goals can tell you a lot about who you are and your progress. Then, you can make direction changes, if any, are needed.

Looking at where you are is not just looking at your actions and accomplishments, but also your values and your dreams. One way to examine your values is to consider unusual views on some of the above issues. The next few sections present more unusual view. As before, you are encouraged to disagree and to think about what *you* believe and why. If you don't know why you think the way you do about a subject, don't forget to try writing about it or discussing it with a friend. You will be amazed at the depth of your own thoughts when you take the time to organize and communicate them.

Gain Self Responsibility

Your faults, especially the ones you deny, are often the cause of your most persistent problems and interfering feelings. If you constantly look for someone or something to blame your problems on, you will never discover these faults. Taking responsibility for everything that has happened to you is how to start to face yourself and find these faults. If you have many faults, it does not mean that you are a worthless person. It might mean that you have taken on more issues in this lifetime than most souls would be willing to tackle. Reviewing your problems in the light of self-responsibility will help you find your faults. Devising a plan or schedule for your personal improvement can aid you in reducing your faults and make you feel better about yourself. Even if you don't get to work on a fault for a while, the fact that you have a plan can allow you to increase your peace of mind right now. Of course this effect will disappear if you don't stick to your plan.

In order to find your faults you can enlist the help of your friends. Ask them to enumerate your qualities – good AND bad. They may be hesitant to do this for you because they suspect that the conversation may turn hostile. Realize that you are asking a lot of them and explain that you will not get defensive. Emphasize your need to know your weaknesses because of your desire to improve yourself. If someone is still uncooperative you can interest them by proposing to tell them things about themselves in an even exchange. They may be interested enough in their image to finally agree. Once they open up, try hard to accept or at least explore their criticisms with inquiries such as: and why do you think that? They may, of course, make criticisms that you believe are based on misunderstandings or incorrect information; resist the temptation to explain or defend yourself. Realize that we often see our actions in the best possible light. Accept that sometimes this light is not so bright.

Can You Avoid Anger?

By now, you understand how anger interferes with intuition, but how do you avoid it if you have the habit? First, understand your own views on anger, then develop them with additional information. Consider that most anger falls one of the following:

1. Excessive frustration
2. Fear
3. Resentment

There are a few things you can use to keep frustration from building up. I keep a pile of bricks and a hammer in my backyard for frustration release. Once, a friend of mine who has a few too many frustrations, found out about it. Even though she was a small person she broke my hammer. That really made her feel good. Let's face it, the cost of a hammer is pretty cheap therapy. When you are really frustrated, it is hard to believe that anything will make you feel better, but hard physical activity where something can be pounded on is a great release. It removes the bad feeling without suppressing it. Strenuous exercise even isometrics can work in a pinch. Another reason to turn frustration into physical activity: as opposed to frustration, it will not kill you. Although, looking at some of the new exercise equipment at my gym, I'm not so sure; some of those machines look like they cold mangle a gorilla.

There are many things that cause anger. Fear is one of the most interesting. The fear of being caught doing something wrong can be a tremendous fear. If a person does get caught, anger is a common and effective defense. Sometimes just knowing about this dynamic, is enough for a person to realize the real cause of their anger and start developing some integrity. Of course, don't hold your breath, often using anger to transfer the guilt is an old behavior that works too well, making these people hopeless.

Overcoming any fear builds character, but how do you over come fear? One thing seems clear: the more often you overcome a fear, the easier it becomes.

Should You Bother to Overcome Your Fears?

Few accomplishments have as strong a reward as overcoming fear. Few accomplishments are as underrated. Overcoming even one of your fears eliminates a situation where your performance, judgement, and intuition can become hindered. Overcoming fear increases your self-confidence which promotes your peace of mind. A major motion picture, starring Merril Streep, called "Defending Your Life," portrayed judgement day as a review of how you handled fear during your life. If you handled fear well, you elevated to the next level of existence. If not, you had to return to Earth and face more fear instilling situations until you overcame them. Although the movie is pure fiction, it brings to life some of the values of overcoming fear.

After overcoming fear, people experience pure joy and a renewed appreciation for freedoms of all types. Daredevils confront their fear over and over again just for the reward of defeating it. There is a little of this devil in all of us. Use him.

Every time you overcome a fear and get through a situation that brings you fear, you weaken that fear. Action overcomes fear even if it does not completely remove it. Overcoming a fear is one of the best things you can do for your self confidence. If you want to try to overcome one, find the most controlled and safe situation to confront your fear. Arrange everything so you have maximum control. Have a couple of friends standing by. Do whatever you need to increase your feeling of confidence then, do the thing you are afraid of. If it is reasonable, do it over and over again. If it involves performing some skill, keep doing it over until the fear stops interfering with your performance. You have truly conquered your fear if you can perform well.

If you want more motivation to confront your fear, remember the horses pushing me around. That experience cost me some self-respect.

76

Your fear could be costing you the respect you deserve. Conquering fear inspires respect in others and in yourself. Overcoming your fear can inspire others to do the same. I'm sure you have been in situations where you have said: "OK, but you go first." Be inspirational; go first.

There is one fear a person should avoid confronting in the above manner: dying. The above manner suggests performing the thing that you fear. So, you see the problem. However, the fear of death can be tremendous. The world often reminds us of this fear. Just driving the freeways reminds us how close death is. A certain amount of fear is reasonable to expect, but your fear of death must be small and set aside most of the time if you are to have peace of mind.

I have a few friends who were very afraid of death. When they confessed this fear I helped them successfully overcome it. All I did was recommend the book, *Life After Life*, by Ray Moody Jr. The book consists of the summarization of hundreds of interviews with people who have died and been revived. The similarities are riveting. You may be amazed at what a little information can do to dispel the darkness of the unknown. Even if you do not fear death, this book is excellent reading for all who are curious about their path in and out of life.

Let me encourage you to conquer a few of your own fears. Last summer I finally relented and let my horsey friend Coleen talk me into going for a little ride "just around the ranch". I remembered my last ride 15 years prior going "just around the barn." It turned out that I had nothing to fear. Riding one of Coleen's horses is like operating an all terrain vehicle with power steering and cruise control. When the ride was over I got down from my horse and it started rubbing its head against me. I pushed it back and we went back and forth for a few minutes – we had become best buddies. All my fear was gone. I had such a feeling of accomplishment; I felt on top of the world for days. Now I look back and realize that my fear had prevented me from enjoying horses for 15 years.

Be encouraged to overcome your fears; many of them are as ill-founded as my horse phobia. Don't let fear cause blocks. This is a terrible waste, especially since fear can, sometimes, be overcome with one confrontation. There are always excuses to help you avoid confronting your fear. When the opportunity presents itself consider the benefits.

Why Bother with Hotheads and Annoying People

Keeping the people around you peaceful helps your own peace of mind. If you know someone who gets angry easily, help them to avoid their anger. When they get angry, talk to them respectfully and ask them if they are aware that they are using an angry voice. If he or she says yes, point out that using an angry voice is beneath them. Tell them that you know they have the smarts to solve the problem without using anger to push the problem away. You can tell them that you want to work with them without placing blame to prevent the problem from escalating. In this way you are promising to protect their ego and at the same time letting them know that you are willing to bring the problem to the attention of your superiors. There are many variations that may work. If they are not aware of their anger, you can tell them how upsetting it is and ask them if they want to do that and volunteer to subtly point it out when they use their angry voice. Talking to the hothead about his or her angry voice every time they use it is better that letting your resentment build and destroying your peace of mind.

Most of you know someone you consider to be totally annoying, totally frustrating. You often become angry when they are around. If you consider yourself superior to this person, you may be right, but then you should be able to change the situation. Consider that the annoyance may be triggered by a particular trait of theirs that you subconsciously recognize and dislike in yourself. Of course, this is not always the case, but if you understand this trigger, you will find opportunities to reduce your anger and simultaneously increase your self-awareness.

Sometimes you have to interact with a truly annoying person who triggers nothing but annoyance. You know that anger hurts your health and your ability to access your intuition, but annoyance comes so quickly when you are around these people. You must learn to get along with them or your intuition may become difficult to access when you are with them and for some time afterwards. There is a method to get along with these people that seems almost magical in its effectiveness. In the morning before you encounter an annoying person, picture them doing or saying something annoying and then visualize yourself rise above the usual reaction of annoyance. Realize that this person must see the reaction they evoke in people, but they can't seem to stop themselves. Set your judgement aside and see yourself trying to understand how hard things must be for this person. Say to yourself: it's OK, I know you have trouble with this. Be ready to let annoyances pass. After a couple minutes of imagery you will be able to avoid your old reaction of annoyance. Then you will be ready for the real thing. You will find that this reaction makes you feel generous and it seems to straighten out that annoying person. When they see that you didn't react negatively to the first annoying thing they do, then they can relax knowing that you may give them a little slack. Applying this imagery to the people who annoy you can eliminate annoyance before it gets started.

Avoid Resentment

When someone commits a serious transgression which causes you to doubt their friendship, consider being truthful: "I feel no obligation to forgive you just because you said sorry. I will wait and see if you actually refrain from treating me with such carelessness." In this manner you can let them know what you think of their actions and give them notice that you refuse to let them treat you like this. Making such statements will prevent resentment from building up and make the relationship more honest or end it.

Resentment creates blocks (see Chapter 3, the section titled Your Body May Motivate You, Sickness) and destroys peace of mind and friendships. Communication is the key to preventing resentment. However, it is difficult to talk to someone about their undesirable traits. On the other hand, if you decide you want a certain person as a friend or lover, you must be able to accept them as they are. Take the bad with the good. Change is difficult. It is not fair or realistic to expect someone to change to suit you. So how do you resolve this dichotomy?

There are two things you can do. One is to accept that you can't get along with everyone. When things happen to people that change them, your relationship may no longer work. If you act with courage at that point, the relationship can become a pleasant memory. If you wait and see, you may be headed towards constant disappointment and pain. Clear communication is the best way to salvage a questionable relationship and at the same time see if it can weather future strains. When your friend exhibits the behavior that bothers you, bring it to their attention. If you don't do this, resentment, the silent destroyer of relationships, will start to grow. What is most important to understand here is that there is a positive way and a negative way to present these things. The positive way can be performed in such a manner that your friends' feelings will be protected. The negative way can seem like an ultimatum.

1. Negative style: Joe, you are my friend and I want to continue being friends, so I want you to know that this bothers me.
2. Positive style: Joe, I value you as a friend just the way you are. You do not have to change, but I want you to know about something that bothers me a bit.

The negative style contains a threat that if Joe doesn't change you are going to discontinue the friendship. This can cause fear and anger. Not a good way to start communicating. The positive style is assuring and will let Joe know that you like him and want him around. Change can happen, but it should be viewed as an unexpected benefit, not a requirement. If you want peace of mind and have difficulty accepting someone the way they are, realize that there are many people out there. You *can* find people who are right for you, but first impressions can be misleading. People are usually on their best behavior when they first meet someone. Their best behavior may be very different from their normal behavior. Therefore, it becomes important to take your time getting to know people, whether they are to become friends or lovers. Whether there is strong chemistry or simple comfort and security, take your time. Take special care when you meet someone who is extremely exciting to be with. Sometimes this excitement is a warning of danger ahead. That person may be dangerous to start a relationship with. There are few things more disquieting to your deeper feelings than a bad relationship.

Don't Forget Your Accomplishments
If you discovered something about yourself while considering some of these issues, write down the discoveries you make. People sometimes make mistakes because they forgot something they learned previously. If you write down the things you learn, they will stay with you longer. You may be amazed at how much pleasure you receive from reading over

your old insights. You may also be amazed at how quickly you forgot those insights.

Although mistakes are a normal part of life and a method of learning, it is most desirable to reduce them and obtain learning from the least painful experiences. Mistakes are often created by selecting the wrong course of action in response to a problem. Therefore, an effective way to reduce your mistakes would be to improve your problem solving skills.

Problem Solving

A person who has the potential to obtain peace of mind knows, at a minimum, that a life without accomplishments and contributions is a poor life. Accomplishments of any significance are usually the result of overcoming problems. Therefore, a significant life is going to have problems. If you see your problems as challenges, then you have the right attitude to produce accomplishments. However, problems can pile up. How can you prevent the discouragement that this brings?

Have you ever walked through the woods and taken a critical look around you? It seems that every leaf appears in the perfect position to create a visual balance. Every twist to each branch seems to be artistically perfect. If you can witness the incredible order of nature, then perhaps you can recognize, that your problems have order and that they are right for your current stage of development. Occasionally people are given problems that completely overwhelm them. This may seem unfair, but it may have order and purpose. The book Messages From Michael by Chelsea Quinn Yarbro presents an interesting explanation for seemingly unjust life situations. If you feel you have such a life, this book may hold a wonderful surprise for you.

Once you have accepted your problems without discouragement, you are half way to developing the right problem solving attitude. If your attitude toward problems is negative, it will be very difficult to turn problems into accomplishments. The right attitude makes solutions come easily, and seems to magically reduce the number of problems that occur.

Most people feel that losing their job is one of the biggest problems that they are likely to face. However, my friends who have been laid off have always landed a better job in a couple of months. The loss of income hardly had any effect on their well-being. I should point out that I pick my friends very carefully. With the exception of one old friend, they are all very positive people. At the moment the exception is living in a high rent area in the heart of Silicon Valley, but commutes an hour each way to get to a low paying job as a technician. He was once an engineer with 30 engineers working under him. He is very bright technically, but he never gets the breaks my other friends always seem to get. They are not any smarter or harder working than he is. However, when he has a problem he always talks about the worst possible outcome. Although he talks in a joking manner and believes he is being entertaining, the outcome he sees reflects his attitude. His negative attitude is the only difference between him and my successful friends.

To place yourself firmly on the road to a successful solution, allow yourself the pleasure of anticipating the good feeling that will accompany solving the problem. The reason for this, strange as it may seem, is that you attract the pictures that you make in your mind. Joking about disastrous outcomes for current problems not only creates the picture in your mind, but also in the minds of your friends. This behavior will get you attention and sympathy, but attracts more disasters. So whenever you catch yourself with a negative thought, replace that thought with the most positive thoughts on the same subject. Spend time loving your dream.

Now that you know what to keep out of your head, consider developing an approach that you can apply to any problem. Consider the approach that follows: It was developed during my work with the Air Force where it was immediately tested on very difficult problems. These problems dealt with jets that the Air Force had given up on. The Air Force doesn't give up easy. They will put three shifts of their own technicians on a problem around the clock before they call in a civilian engineer. The problems they gave me had already beaten men with four or five years of experience. All I had was five weeks of reading manuals like The Theory of Operation.

Despite my inexperience, and lack of training, I gained the respect of the technicians and pilots with whom I worked. The squadrons where I worked consistently had the best maintenance record in the entire Air Force for the systems I supported. The only way I could do that was to always solve the problem, no matter what. This success was not accomplished by obtaining knowledge. It was accomplished by developing a problem solving approach and maintaining the right attitude. The correct attitude is the most important aspect of problem solving so it is presented first.

Feel the Light
Use this first variation of the Feel the Light tool for developing the best attitude for problem solving:

1. Whenever you are confronted by a problem or a difficult situation, imagine you have just found the solution and allow yourself to feel the elation of a brilliant solution; one that makes things even better than before the problem. Actually see yourself in the future and fill in as many details as you can think of. The details should support the physical scene as well as the idea that the solution was efficient and effective. Remember to maintain that feeling of success as you picture the scene. This tool is call "matching the feeling of success".
2. At the same time, imagine yourself filling up with a golden light.
3. Imagine that the color inside you is the feeling of success.
4. Blend the feeling with the color until they become one.

   Images have a strong effect on how we feel. After you have used the above tool a few times, you may be able to picture yourself filled with golden light and the feeling of success will flow into your body. Your ability to do this depends on your peace of mind.
   Matching and then monitoring the feelings you have created (feeling the light) is the fundamental part of the tool you will be taught for accessing your intuition. Therefore, developing a problem solving attitude by feeling the light will sharpen your intuitive skills and should be performed as often as possible. Filling yourself with the golden light of success and performing the rest of the technique will help you sail over the troubled seas of life.
   One method to maintain peace of mind is to recognize each problem as a stimulus for achievement and improvement. We need achievements to feel good about ourselves. Therefore happiness and problems go hand and hand. The difference between really happy people and people who

must distract themselves to feel happy is not how many problems they have, but their attitude towards their problems.

When I was a systems engineer, I spend most of my time solving difficult technical problems that would, sometimes, take days to get a handle on. Problems tended to pile up. A lot of problems without solutions can wear a person down. As a defense, I developed some additional tools for solving problems. Once I realized that these new tools combined with the right attitude made solutions appear easily, I was able to work more comfortably, knowing that no matter what I was up against, I had a complete approach to finding the solution ready to use as soon as I needed it.

Complete Problem Solving Procedure

Some problems can be clearly recognized as requiring some special effort, having a good idea of what the effort is going to be will greatly reduce worry and increase your chances of success. The following procedure has taken the fear out of the tough problems and allowed me to feel good regardless of my problems.

1. Know the problem well. Review the details of the problem until you have each one memorized.
2. Perform the success matching tool, feel the light.
3. While continuing to match the feeling of success and experiencing the golden light, perform a simple, menial task that requires no thought. Relax as deeply as you can during this task. Performing this menial task will allows your subconscious to work on the problem. Your subconscious is your best problem solver, but you must relax and clear your mind in order to hear or see the solution when it comes up.
4. Allow yourself to be convinced that an excellent solution will be found.

Avoid:

1. Thinking that the problem is impossible. Avoid this no matter how difficult the problem appears.

2. Worrying. Do not visualize negative outcomes. If you catch yourself in this trap, picture the most positive outcome for twice as long. Embrace it. Say: wouldn't it be wonderful if we solved this problem today?

As previously stated, the problems you are given may represent a challenge designed just for you. If you want to realize the truth in this statement, observe the problems of others, not your own.

Performing a simple task while maintaining a relaxed state of mind is an important part of the problem solving approach. Some people have learned on their own that certain activities like taking a drive help them solve problems. This is because difficult problems are solved in our subconscious mind, and the connection between the subconscious and the conscious is tenuous. A person's failure to remember parts of a dream they just had is an example of this tenuous connection. Menial, boring tasks bring on dreamlike thought patterns and the conscious mind recedes. The subconscious can then come forward with the solution. The appearance of the solution is so stimulating that it "wakes up" your conscious mind which latches onto it. The solution appears to come from nowhere because the subconscious recedes, just like when you wake after a dream.

It can take as long as fifteen minutes for the subconscious mind to come forward, especially if you have trouble relaxing. This is why taking a drive works so well: it is easy to do, and driving for fifteen minutes or more is not an excessive amount of time. It is, however, a long time to just sit while trying to make a solution appear.

A good problem solving approach can prevent a person from feeling overwhelmed when a few problems appear, but what can you do when tons of problems appear?

Problem Solving Philosophy

Attitude is essential. Feeling the light creates a high and positive energy level, but sometimes problems overwhelm us so that we get too emotional and can't control our negativity. At times like this it is helpful to review the most serious problems of a year or two ago. Recall how serious those problems seemed to you at that time. Now compare that to how serious those old problems seem from today's point of view. It is likely that they no longer seem so bad. If you can look at today's problems from an objective distance, they too will not seem so bad.

The right attitude can take the negative power of a problem and turn it into positive power. This is one of the fundamental beliefs of Eastern thinking and the reason why some such thinkers can meet disaster with such calm: great disaster creates great potential for good fortune. Maintaining a good attitude is the catalyst that changes disaster into good fortune. Some call it the pendulum effect. As you use your problem solving procedure, imagine that you can take the negative swing and ride it far into the positive side ending up in a better position than before.

The next time you think, "this is a big problem", quickly start looking for ways to turn the big problem into a big opportunity and picturing the best possible outcome. You can turn any problem around and use it to your advantage. It may look impossible at first, but attitude, action, and amusement can change that.

You can use the following true observations to maintain the right attitude:

1. Many problems seem impossible to solve.
2. 99% of these problems have solutions.
3. It is very difficult to distinguish the truly impossible 1% from the apparently impossible 99%.

The secret to solving problems is to recognize that most challenging problems seem impossible until the very last instant before either the solution rises from your subconscious or someone with a better problem solving attitude tells you the solution. If you want to find these solutions yourself, develop the best possible attitude and avoid doing things like worrying.

There is an interesting story about man who finds a bottle with a genie inside. The genie tells him he can have whatever he wants provided that the most evil man in the world got double. After thinking for a while, the man realizes that all his wishes would give the most evil man in the world too much power. Finally, he laughs and says that this is a hard problem. Then he gets an idea, "Give me ten million dollars and beat me half to death." Did you think of that solution? See, there are all sorts of solutions that don't appear right away.

Some people don't want solutions. Solutions almost always require action and eliminate the attention and sympathy that problems that these people want. These people are easy to recognize; they mostly talk about their problems and they have a lot of them.

If nature takes such obvious care with the biological systems of its creatures to create such wonders as the human body, it is just possible that care is put into every aspect of creation even fate. Therefore, it is possible that problems are given to you for specific reasons. Perhaps to improve your character and gain wisdom or simply to make you stronger. If you view problems with this attitude, you will find them easier to solve, and gain knowledge and confidence from the experience. Don't forget to write down what you learned from your more challenging problems.

When you are confronted with a problem you must take some action or the negative feelings associated with it are likely to create a block. Sometimes all that is necessary is to make a plan. The plan might be that you will work on the problem at a certain time and place and until then you will picture a positive outcome for the problem. It only takes a little time to make a plan, but even if the plan requires hard work in the future, just having the plan and the commitment to carry it out can help your peace of mind. Of course, to avoid a future block you must follow your plan. For that you need motivation.

Motivation

Or Strange Idea #22

Putting off a problem by making a plan is easy, but when that time rolls around, what is going to make you do the required work? If many people know that the problem is your responsibility, you have concern for your reputation to help motivate you. However, when few people or only yourself know about the problem, all you have is your integrity to motivate you. For many people this is not enough.

If you believe you have integrity but are ignoring your problems, then you are proving the statement that the easiest person to fool is yourself. You must get your act together regarding your problems if you are to have the calmness of mind to use your intuition. To have peace of mind, you must learn to love, honor, and respect yourself. If you shirk the commitments you make to yourself, it becomes difficult to have the self-respect from which peace of mind grows.

What is more important to you, the image you have of yourself (self-respect) or the image others have of you? Look at the way you dress. Do you care about your appearance? Avoid unfashionable clothes? People see themselves in the mirror, fully dressed, for about one minute a day. It is unlikely that you are trying to look good because you like to see yourself look good for one minute. You are dressing to present an image to others. Now look around at the inside of your home, your car, your office. This is what you see most of the time. This is a part of you that you present to yourself. It affects the image you have of yourself. Is it as neat and clean as you make yourself appear? Are you more concerned with what others see of you than what you see of yourself? Most everybody is. Very few will admit it. If your self image is not important to you it becomes difficult to maintain confidence and avoid worry. Care of our self image is an essential part of loving ourselves.

There is an interesting paradox concerning self image: many of us are more concerned about the image we project to others than we are about how we feel about ourselves, yet the people whose thoughts we are concerned with are not thinking about how nice we are or how smart we are or how good we look. They are thinking, about their own image. Almost nobody is thinking about us, or about the image we present to them. They are only thinking about how they appear. If you can recognize this attitude, you will have a valuable tool for getting along with people. You will stop trying to control what people are thinking about you and start spending more time developing the opinion you have of yourself, the one that counts the most.

Hypnosis for Motivation

Image can be a powerful motivator, but it is still easy to get wrapped up in the events of the day and forget your plans. It is easy to forget. An automatic reminder/motivator would be a wonderful resource. It turns out that one exists. It's called hypnosis. This form of motivation has many additional benefits. One is stress reduction. Stress reduction helps people to improve their health, sleep soundly, and develop a general feeling of well-being. However, seeing a hypnotist to motivate you to work on your day-to-day problems may be a bit extreme. There is a less extreme method and the price is right: self-hypnosis. Perhaps a more accurate term for the following tool would be friend hypnosis. I personally believed hypnosis to be such an effective and worthwhile tool that I became a certified hypnotherapist. I was surprised to learn that hypnosis is neither difficult to learn nor dangerous to practice. Hypnosis for motivation can be learned from a book. The subjects only needs to posses some level of suggestibility and feel comfortable in each other's company. The best person to practice hypnosis with is an old friend with whom you share a well established relationship.

Before starting out on your exploration of the suggestibility of your subconscious mind, a few concepts regarding hypnosis need to be understood. Hypnosis is a natural state of mind. Most people experience this state a couple of times a week. Monotonous activities such as jogging and driving can bring on an hypnotic state. Driving home without recalling some parts of the trip is indicative of having been in a mild hypnotic state. There is nothing complicated about going into a hypnotic state. It occurs naturally when the subconscious mind comes forward and the conscious mind steps down or "goes to sleep". We can operate perfectly well with our subconscious mind. It might even be better suited than the conscious mind for driving because it is more intuitive and might sense a dangerous situation and thus cause you to slow down and avoid an accident. Unfortunately, your subconscious mind is extremely gullible. It needs the judgment abilities of the conscious mind to protect it from the outside world. Like all things, there needs to be balance between using the conscious and the subconscious minds. In order to maintain this balance it helps to understand something about their relationship.

The reason some people don't remember part of a hypnotic session or part of the drive home is that the connection between the subconscious and the conscious minds is so tenuous. In other words, the conscious mind sends information to the subconscious that is clear and easy for the subconscious mind to understand. However, the communication from the subconscious to the conscious mind can be very unclear. Often this communication consists of only momentary feelings or fleeting images. Your dreams are a perfect example of this communication. If you are like most people, you have trouble remembering your dreams. This is because you dream with your subconscious. When you wake, your conscious mind takes over. At that point, you must use the communication link from the conscious *to* the subconscious mind in order to remember the dream.

The dream state is a good example of another feature of the relationship between these two states of mind. When you are dreaming, you think that everything is normal, even though you may be doing very unusual things, like flying through the air. The gullible subconscious mind is actually thinking that you are in the waking state and that everything is normal despite the fact that there is nothing under your feet. It is not until you wake up that you realize that you were dreaming. Under hypnosis, just as in a dream, you may not notice any difference from your waking state until you come out of hypnosis. Only then will you realize how pleasantly different you felt. You may also notice that you sleep more deeply and wake up feeling better for the next few days.

Some people feel that they will not be in control when they are hypnotized. This is not true. In the hypnotic state, as in the dream state, you will make judgments just as you would in your waking state. Like the dream state, you will probably believe that you are awake. Therefore, you will not tell anyone things you do not want them to know, and you will not do anything that is against your nature. You will always be in control despite the fact that you may not remember parts of a hypnotic session, just like you don't remember parts of a dream. This fact is recognized by the American Bar Association and the courts of our country. Even if a person can prove that they were hypnotized, they are still responsible for their actions.

Getting back to self-hypnosis. There are a number of books on the subject, but self-hypnosis can be a difficult task. The problem is that a person must remain conscious enough to remember the goal of the session and at the same time release the conscious mind sufficiently to allow the subconscious mind to come forward. Making a hypnosis tape is a much easier method, but some people get distracted when they listen to their own voice. They start to notice minor flaws in their speech. To avoid this happening, it is better to have a tape made by a friend that's friend hypnosis.

The person who is reading should also be able to feel kindness and concern for the person who will listen to the tape. The reader should feel these emotions and put them into their voice as they read, much like the tone used to soothe an upset child. Reading with a monotonous rhythm will add to the soothing effect. The goal is to make the person who is being hypnotized feel as comforted and secure as possible. The next task is to write the hypnotic suggestions that will create motivation. Refer to Appendix A for a few suggestions.

Once the appropriate suggestions are developed and written out, it is time to make the tape. The induction in Appendix B is just one example of many possibilities.

If you wish to learn how to use hypnosis to make changes in your life or obtain goals, find a book on hypnosis. Most such book are full of different suggestions. You may want to combine pieces from a number of suggestions and work them into a customized suggestion for yourself or a friend. As you learn more you will be amazed at how many aspects of your life can be improved with hypnosis. Even medical problems and difficult conditions like warts respond to hypnosis. The more visual a problem is, the better it is suited for hypnosis. I had a couple of stubborn warts I called Fred and Ed which shrunk to nothing after I started using hypnosis on them.

The activity of following a hypnotic induction, like the one in Appendix B not only helps motivation, but will also put you in the right mental state to access your subconscious mind where the solutions to problems can be found. If you want to use hypnosis to help find solutions, make a special tape that has more details of the walk down the path and many details of your special place. The only suggestion should be a reassurance that all problems have solutions and that you only need to fill yourself with the golden light of success, relax, and enjoy your special place. You can use this tape as your reward tape and use it when you want to be good to yourself. We all need a mini-vacation at least a couple of times a week and a reward tape is a simple and practical way to get that vacation, reduce stress, or solve problems.

Dependability and Blocks

Or Strange Idea #23

You are not an island. Everyday someone – your friends, colleagues or family is depending on you. If you disappoint them, an apology may get you a reprieve, but you may still feel inadequate or even guilty. Although these feelings may not be very obvious, they can collect to form a block to your intuition. One way to prevent a block from forming in this situation is to commit to making amends when the opportunity arises, amends in the form of actions, not just words. Of course the best way to avoid these types of blocks is to be dependable in all your relations. Perhaps all that a person needs in order to improve their dependability is some additional motivation.

Motivation to be dependable can be found in the negative and positive aspects of your interactions with people. On the negative side, when we let people down and then apologize, almost everybody will say it's OK, even though it is often not what they really feel. Although in many cases the apology will seem to work, in actuality you will have generated resentment that may permanently affect a person's regard for you.

A positive motivation for dependability can come from your friends and colleagues. Ask them what qualities they admire the most in people. You will find that dependability is often very close to the top of the list. Think about the people you admired. Would you say that they were dependable? Now think about the best friends you ever had. Were they dependable? Finally, how much stress could you remove from your life history by eliminating the interactions of those who have proven to be undependable? We are attracted to charming people, but dependable people are the real treasures of life.

For most of us, life contains many obligations and responsibilities, and still we want to enjoy ourselves. Everybody I know is so busy that they need two week's notice to get together on a weekday. With so many things to do it is easy to forget an appointment. Forgetting to do something is usually how most people fail in their attempt to be dependable. It would help a person's dependability to keep an appointment book with them at all times. This isn't always easy, especially for men who don't carry a purse. One solution is to use the back of an old business card and keep it in your wallet. On the left side write down the days of the week. Use the space just to the right of each day for any appointments you have that do not occur during work hours. On the other side of your card you can usually find space to make a list of the people that you need to call and cross them off as you contact them. Perhaps the business card method seems a bit excessive, but keeping appointments in your head is a good place to lose them as well as your dependability.

Stress Stopper

Or Strange Idea #24

If you are feeling pressured because you have too much work, don't get stressed, get organized. You will be more relaxed as you work because you can rely on your plans to keep track of what needs to be done. Devise your own organization or use a to-do list. Write down everything you need to do leaving an inch before each task and skip lines between tasks. In front of each task draw a box. Outside the box, place a priority number from one to ten, and the necessary completion date. When you have taken care of the task, put a line through the box and, if appropriate, write down the final disposition on the line below the task. These lists can make you feel good about your work because you will be able to see the many things you have accomplished. Usually people are so aware of the things they need to do that they easily forget what they have completed and they feel that they aren't going anywhere. If you use a computer to make your to-do list, you can transfer all the tasks you have accomplished into a draft of your annual review input.

You might think that you don't have time to make a to-do list. If that is what you think then you need a to-do list more than most. To-do lists give you a chance to have more time by presenting a method of organizing. They also give you a chance to relax. You can let go of some tension just by thinking that at least you have it written down on your list. You have to start relaxing somehow and starting is often the hardest part. Once you start to relax you may need a bit of will to let go of the things that stress does for you. Let go of the importance, the special attention and consideration that being stressed can bring. Be brave enough to relax and trust that you can handle what comes at you without the attention and concern from your loved ones.

A to-do list can be a real life saver, especially when you have failed to do something. You can demonstrate that it was not forgotten because it was on your list, but hopefully it was given a low priority which, combined with time constraints, prevented its accomplishment. In this way the list can be used to get you additional help by showing your boss all the tasks you have and how many of them must be delayed if he is adding to it without getting you some help.

If you have enlightened management, you probably have weekly one-on-ones with your boss. With some bosses these should be called one-on-none. This is where the to-do list is most helpful. In preparation you can find the to-do list items that will solve a problem (these items are really solutions to these problems). During your one-on-one, show your boss the problems that these solutions relate to and *then* the "solutions" you plan to implement. Leave a few unsolved problems for your boss to suggest solutions to (bosses have to have something to do or they'll get into trouble). If your boss suggests a few changes to your solutions, try to support these changes. This makes the task part of your bosses responsibility and you may get more support.

Many jobs entail a large number of small interruptions and unexpected problems. It is easy to get behind under these circumstances. Few things are more pressure building than being late all the time, but how do you compensate for interruptions? To avoid this predicament, be more conservative when estimating completion dates for longer tasks. This will leave you time to handle those unforeseen interruptions. If you need help in establishing a more conservative estimating gauge, try this for a day or two:

1. Note the start and stop time for the periods you work on your scheduled tasks.
2. When you are interrupted, even for a minute, write down the number of minutes.
3. At the end of this period, add up the actual time you are able to put into scheduled tasks per day.

Use that amount of time as a basis for estimating completion dates.

You may think this new conservative estimating would make you appear an underachiever. But actually it allows you to appear as someone who completes their tasks on time. Avoid trying to be impressive by volunteering to complete a large task quickly. It is more likely that you will impress people if you tell them that you are so busy (and therefore, important) that you can't get to something until next week, next month, or until you get a really good looking assistant. If you want to impress people with your speed, do it on small jobs. Whenever you are interrupted and asked to do some short task, do it immediately. This is impressive and costs you very little since you will have to do it pretty soon anyway.

If your new conservative completion date is too late for your requesters to accept, hold your ground. Avoid agreeing to "try" to finish something early. This is the same as agreeing to their date. They will expect it on their date and consider you late if you don't make this "try" date. You also subject yourself to more pressure from them because they think they will have to push you to finish it by a date you thought was too soon. If a manager insists on some unreasonable date tell them, "I will perform whatever task you want, and I will do it your way, but if you ask me when it will be finished, I will tell you the truth." Or, if you want to be a little stronger, " You manage resources, people, time, and schedules; I know you are a good manager. I am telling you the reality of the time involved with this task. You manage the rest and together we will perform, like a team." They love that teamwork talk. Now you may have a little extra time at work. You must give yourself extra time or you could find yourself working long hours to try and catch up. The problem with contributing your own time to a project is that it is now personal. If the project is canceled you will feel that you have wasted your own personal time. Some people love their work, but anything you spend 40 hours a week doing, you are doing enough. There is an amazing world out there that can enrich your life and have a profound effect on who you are. Try spending time doing things that are as different from your work as you can find, with people that are as different from your colleagues as possible. This puts your work in prospective and prevents work problems from becoming the end of the world.

Avoid selecting friends from the people at work. There are many reasons why this is a bad policy; just one of them is that you will have less time to finish your work because of friend related interruptions.

You may be thinking, "Great, now I have more things to do, and I still haven't learned what I have to do to relieve my stress I didn't manage to avoid." The good news is that eliminating that stress is not difficult, if you are willing to spend 15 minutes a couple of times a week. The best news is that during this fifteen minutes you don't have to do anything except relax and listen. The initial effort will be to follow the directions in the Motivation section of chapter 4, Obtaining Peace of Mind, for making an hypnosis tape and add the stress reduction suggestions to the other suggestions you select. Suggested suggestions are located in Appendix A. When I was a hypnotherapist, patients often commented on one long lasting effect of being hypnotized: reduced stress. Besides this benefit, hypnosis offers a number of job performance enhancing features. When it comes to relieving stress, hypnosis *is* the magic pill with no side effects. A close second is love. If you don't have a special person to love how about yourself? How about loving your life?

Love Your Life

Or Strange Idea #25

I love to get together with my friends and tell stories or just chatter about the more exciting things that are happening in my life, but I have one friend, Rita, with whom I hardly say a word. I let her do all the talking even though she mostly talks about herself. We don't have much in common, she is the mother of two teenagers, while I am a confirmed bachelor, and we come from different generations. Nevertheless, I have doggedly maintained contact with her for eight years.

You might think that someone who talks mostly about themselves would be bragging or complaining, but Rita doesn't appear to do either. You might think that someone who doesn't encourage others to talk would appear selfish, but Rita seems generous and concerned. The reason for these apparent contradictions is that when Rita talks you can hear and actually feel the tremendous love she has for her life. It radiates from her, and basking in its warmth is a great pleasure.

This love of life attracts people to Rita, makes positive things happen, and allows her to change adversity into advantage. One example is her house. Rita lives in the Santa Cruz Mountains near the epicenter of the big earthquake that shook San Francisco in 1989. Her house was actually a summer home without heat or adequate insulation. As an afterthought, a wood burning stove was added but it was still a cold place in which to live. The quake damaged the foundation enough to require replacement. The house had to be replaced, although she could live in it until construction or destruction commenced. With the help of an inexpensive loan from the federal emergency relief fund Rita now has a new house with central heating, good insulation and her monthly mortgage payment is $200 less.

I have a friend, Larry, who is quite introspective. He has spent a lot of time in self exploration, knows himself well, and has learned what he needs to feel content. He does what he loves: he teaches gymnastics to earn a living and composes and edits music to fulfill his creative needs. You have undoubtedly heard his work if you watch gymnastics or ice-skating on TV. He has his niche and found a bit of peace of mind. As a gymnastics instructor he is compassionate with his students. He doesn't pressure them; he encourages them. He, like myself, views gymnastics as an art, an art of appreciation for how our bodies can spin and fly. This relaxed attitude results in some criticism from his boss, who wants to have a team of national champions. One day his boss got frustrated with Larry's relaxed attitude and told Larry that he was nothing. What his boss was really saying was that Larry had no championship team, no high paying job, no fancy car...

Larry just smiled and said "Maybe that's why I'm happy."

If you can learn to love your life, positive things will start to happen and you will take a giant step towards peace of mind. To develop a love of life, take a lesson from Rita, think on the positive events of your life and talk about the good things that happen to you and not about your problems. You will only appear to be bragging if you speak with the intention of impressing people, but not if you speak from the love you have for your life.

Relaxation and Energy

Or Strange Idea #26

If you don't have fifteen minutes to listen to a hypnosis tape, can you give yourself a twenty second stress-relief moment? Considering all the hours you give to work, taking twenty seconds to reduce your nervous energy output spend should not be difficult. Although such a moment can be very effective, it is difficult to remember. Wrist watches that beep on the hour are one way of reminding yourself to take a moment. If you care too much about your job and not enough about yourself, you may not be able to devise rewards or create stress-relief moments. Is this you? Ask a friend.

The Stress-relief Moment

This twenty second stress-relief moment needs one prop: a picture of a beautiful natural scene without any people. Locate this picture so it is always in your field of view. Perform this simple exercise every hour or two:

1. Sit-up straight and look at the picture.
2. Rotate each shoulder, one at a time, forward, up, back and down, while breathing deeply.
3. RELAX.

There are many forms of stress relief. When I was studying to get through college, I agreed to let myself play guitar for 10 minutes if I studied for 50. I was a little loose with my timing so I almost flunked out of college but, I did become a darn good guitar player. That reward has now become a daily morning ritual that rarely fails to lift my spirits. You can find something that relieves your stress and becomes just as enjoyable if you are truly willing to give up your stress.

If you have a little more time during the day, but not enough for a full 15 minutes to listen to a tape, you can heal your stress damage by performing the Block Removing tool in chapter 6, Block Busters. When you are finished with this book, you will have an arsenal of stress relieving tools. As a matter of fact, you may be too relaxed to hold the book. When you start using these tools, you may find that you have more energy. However, stagnation, lack of interest, or lack of stimulation can prevent you from noticing your new energy.

If you work at a desk all day, what sort of break should you take? Should you go sit somewhere and drink something you can easily drink at your desk? How do you revitalize? The "tired" feeling most people get at work is often stagnation due to a lack of stimulation. If you want to accomplish more with your break time, find ways to get your blood pumping. Take a walk around the building or help a friend in the warehouse. But, it should be as different from your usual position and actions as possible.

Most people are willing to spend five or ten minutes at work in idle chatter, but wouldn't spend two minutes to relieve their stress. Where is their sense of value? You can't have peace of mind if you are stressed out; you can, however, perform your job worse and damage your health. Responding to pressure by getting organized, working more carefully, and doing relaxation techniques promotes peace of mind and prevents mistakes. Mistakes are the real time wasters and pressure makers on most projects. If you maintain conservative completion dates and learn to work relaxed, you will make fewer mistakes.

Worry and the Worriers

Or Strange Idea #27

Besides causing mammoth blocks, worrying increases the likelihood of the negative outcome. Worry is such a tremendous and underrated destructive force that it deserves a new name, something more impressive, a name that tells of its destructive power. Every time you think, say, or hear the word worry, immediately think or say: negative visualization. If someone is talking and they mention the word worry, you can say: oh yes, negative visualization. People are often inspired by this insight the very first time they hear it. Be inspirational. Someday you may make a big difference in someone's life.

When you suspect that someone has been worrying about you, which is sometimes the same as knowing that your mother is awake, confront them with the damage they are doing to your efforts: "So, you have been doing negative visualization about me again. If you are really concerned about my welfare, picture my success. If you continue to do negative visualization against me, I will know that you are entertaining yourself at my expense, and will strive to keep you out of my affairs." If they say, "Do you think I like to worry about you?" you can point out that disasters get much more attention on TV news than any positive human interest story. The destruction of one's career may not be as exciting as a train wreck, but in both cases the attraction is formed from the same elements.

This may be a stern attitude to take, but worry hurts the negative visualizer as well as the subject of the worry. If you want a more passive approach, don't tell these people anything that they can worry about. Only tell them about good things that happen to you. Never tell them about anything you are going to do that has some risk.

If you catch yourself engaging in a negative visualization, stop and practice a positive visualization on the same subject for at least twice as long. If you find yourself doing negative visualization often, try to find out why you want failure. The most common reason is that failure gets attention from our friends and family. Getting attention as a result of our problems is sometimes the only form of love a person experiences. This is such a common trap that you may need an active program to avoid this form of love. How about a substitution? How about love of life?

You can use problems to bring attention and love into your life. Or, you can love and relive your successes, both past and future. You can love yourself through loving your life and attract other forms of love to yourself. You can love your future successes by daydreaming the achievement of your goals. But, not all goals promote peace of mind.

Goals Worth Dreaming About

Or Strange Idea #28

People who work themselves to death so they can get the big house, fancy cars, or just one more promotion are often after false happiness. These people are operating under the mistaken assumption that the goal they seek will make them happy. Unfortunately, the actual achievement of many goal seems to greatly diminish its value. Consider this: if the actions you take to achieve your goals do not satisfy your need to

100

contribute, to be creative, to learn, or to enjoy your life more fully, then you may have chosen the wrong goals. It is as important to enjoy the *process* as it is to value *what* you achieve.

Once you have established goals whose requirements are worthy actions, you may want to check your attitude:

1. Avoid wanting or thinking in a way that is similar to wanting.
2. Adjust your thought processes so that your thoughts are basically appreciation: "Wouldn't it be *wonderful* if I achieved this goal?

If you examine how you feel when you are wanting things, you may notice a slight background feeling similar to fear. That feeling comes from worry, the worry of not getting what you are wanting. Spending time in appreciation, in love, of how nice it will be when you have obtained something, is a powerful positive visualization. It is sometimes called daydreaming by the people who do it habitually. If you succeed in substituting daydreaming for wanting, you may notice a significant change in your life. The things you would love to have happen to you, may start happening. Remember my little gray toy fighter?

To be really happy you need to deal with how you feel when you are not distracted. Learn how to remove the old junk inside of you and fix the issues that exist in the tangible world. When I applied these ideas to my own life, I was presented with an undeniable conclusion. I realized that I needed to treat people better. After more experimenting I found an approach that had better results than any other. From the first moment I would meet someone, even if it was a cashier at the market, I would look for something to love in them. I could find something to love in almost anybody. It was easy and it generated a wonderful response in others. If I failed to find something I could love in a person I simply kept away from them. This also proved to be an excellent policy.

When I found someone I needed to keep away from, my usual reaction, after moving away, was to entertain myself by thinking clever but critical things about them. Things like: learn from your parents' mistakes, use birth control. The problem was that these thoughts left me feeling pretty bad. I soon realized that moving away physically wasn't enough. I tried to stop the critical thoughts by attempting to put the person out of my mind. When I succeeded, I would feel much better. I soon realized that I had to move away physically and mentally from that person. The only problem came when this unpleasant person was someone at work.

If there was someone at work who was impossible to love even in the slightest way, I couldn't move away without changing my job. First, I tried to stop thinking critically about them. Then I started to think about what an accomplishment it would be to get along with them. In the morning before work I would picture myself getting along with them and imagine myself responding to their usual bad behavior with patience. Then, I would go to work and without any real action on my part, we would get along beautifully. The only problem that happened afterwards was that these creepy people wanted to be my friend.

Sometimes people can be so socially unaware that it is very hard to be patient with them. Fortunately, I realized something that made it much easier to have patience and understanding with the most unpleasant of people: it is just possible that no matter how much of a jerk someone is, I might have become just like them if everything that happened to them, from birth until now, happened to me. I also realized that these people suffer. They see the reaction on the faces of the people who they offend, but they usually can't help being products of their environment. Therefore, these unpleasant people deserved my compassion, not my contempt. Condemning someone will rob you of your peace of mind; however, it can make you feel self-righteous. That is an enticing trap because self-righteousness feels good; you feel good because you believe you are so much better that that other person. But, eventually that self-righteous feeling is replaced by emptiness. Is this you? Ask a friend.

Once I adopted the above attitudes and awareness', my relations with people improved tremendously. I developed a fairly consistent feeling of peace which allowed me to be more sensitive to my deeper feelings. Eventually, this sensitivity pointed out a few things I still needed to do for myself. I realized I needed to feel accomplishments. I am and always have been a problem solver. I discovered that I needed the challenge of new problems and the confidence that they would be overcome. I needed to create things with my hands. And for the long run, I needed to do things to constantly improve my character. As the years have past and my conversations with friends have become more introspective, I realize that almost everybody has these same needs. Is this you also? This

102

sounds like a question only you can answer, but talking it over with a friend can still help.

Friends

Or Strange Idea #29

Previously, ideas have been presented for your examination. It was not important whether you agreed or disagreed with these ideas. They were intended to stimulate your awareness of your own feelings on the subject. The eventual purpose was to have you discover, among other things, your own sense of values. The subject of friends, however, will be presented with a very different purpose in mind. This information is presented as an essential truth regardless of who you are or what else you believe. There is no peace of mind without friends. There is no real happiness without friends. There is no security without friends. There is, however, tremendous emptiness when you don't have any friends. That emptiness is easily and sometimes desperately filled with whatever is handy. Unfortunately, negativity is very handy and effective.

Millions of dollars are spent each year to combat depression and anxiety. Drugs, psychiatrists, psychologists, and counselors are used in a struggle that can often be alleviated by a few good friends.

One year, I had a stubborn injury. Eventually, I had to stop my gymnastics, swimming and windsurfing which had allowed me to release the minor frustrations of my life. I also had to stop playing guitar and piano. My music had brightened practically every morning for thirty years. The impact of these losses was more severe than I thought possible. My frustration level would soar at a the slightest inconvenience. I often felt tremendously angry for no apparent reason. I really thought that I would find myself in jail after punching someone for some inconsequential offense. During this time, certain words uttered by my friends put my spirits back on track again and again. It is a wonderful feeling to have someone say, "You don't sound too good, are you OK?" And, I know I made their day when I told them the truth, "I have been feeling down, but your sensitivity and concern has really cheered me up." During these years my friends were tremendously consistent with their concern and support. What could have been a totally terrible year turned out to warm my heart.

I do not have wonderful friends because I'm such a great person. Actually, I'm real annoying. I have way too much energy and I analyze everything to death. I have wonderful friends because when it comes to my sense of values, friends are at the very top. Friends help us see ourselves more clearly. Though we can easily fool ourselves, friends are not so easily fooled. Without them we could be victims of our own illusion. If we are sick, friends can take away the pain. They can heal our wounds. If we are lost, friends can show us a way out that escaped our frantic searching. As a result of these attitudes, I put great effort into making friends with the exceptional people I met and keeping in contact with them. I am still in contact with friends I made before I could walk. This gives me a sense of security. I know that in my old age I will always have friends around to annoy.

Of course to maintain a good friendship you need to be a good friend. A good friend is many things besides dependable and considerate. Good friends resist blaming others for their problems and they care for others with action, not lip service. Perhaps you are good at maintaining a friendship but have trouble finding good friends. Keeping a friend is one thing. Finding a friend is something else entirely.

Good friends are hard to find and they often have too many friends already. A person can have too many friends because real friendships require time and energy – two things of which we all have limited amounts. We must select friends wisely and not make friends with people who just happen to be nearby.

Bad Friends

The easiest people to make friends with are at work. This way you can keep in contact with little effort and actually get paid for it. However, there are many problems with developing friendships with your colleagues. Below are only a few:

1. Associating with the same people all the time reduces the variety of subjects, opinions, and ideas that you are exposed to.

2. Working and socializing with the same people increases the risk of overexposure. Those little things that normally don't bother you about a person can, with overexposure, become annoying. This will put a strain on your friendship *and* add stress to your work place.
3. Friends interact in more way than colleagues interact. This increases the chances for a misunderstanding to get out of hand. This can destroy the friendship and the professional respect and cooperation you once had. Professional interactions with that person can become very uncomfortable after you lose the friendship.
4. If you are in a position to make promotions and you have a friend among the candidates, you are in a no win position. Your friend will be upset with you if he or she is not promoted and if you promote your friend, others will suspect you of favoritism.

If you want smooth sailing at the work place, keep away from busy waters.

Making Good Friends

The best way to make friends is during your favorite activities whether they be athletic, intellectual, or cultural. The best potential friends are often members of the opposite sex. This may be due to the fact that, in the past their lovers have been training them to be more considerate towards members of the opposite sex. Such friendships often pose an obvious question: should you have sex with them? Here are a few things to consider:

1. A person who wishes to be happy can do without a lover but not without friends.
2. Platonic friendships seem to last forever, even longer than friendships between the same sexes, while all but the most exceptional romances burn out in a few years.
3. If you realize that a new friend doesn't have all the attributes that will keep you interested and passionate for a significantly long time, think twice. Here is somebody that might make a life long friend. Becoming lovers and breaking it off after a short time could make you a life-long antagonist.

4. A person with many close friends finds the prospect of old age a lot less scary.

When I traveled around for Hughes Aircraft I moved every year or two. When I arrived in a new location I had to quickly search for friends. Therefore, when I saw somebody I thought was my kind of person I had strong motivation to approach them. I know this is hard for most people. It was hard for me too, but the more you do it the easier it becomes. The best thing to do is make a comment about something that is present. For instance in a book store, "If you aren't looking for anything specific, I read this book once and I loved it." If they will ask you about the book, you know they are interested in talking to you. If they thank you for the suggestion, you know it is time to smile and beat it out of there. If they say they are looking for some particular book you can ask them why they liked it.

There are books on opening lines, but the best line I have heard was from a very funny guy. He walked up to a woman in a supermarket and said; "So how do you like me so far?" They are together now and seem to have a good relationship. If you are new in an area, you have a built-in line, "Hi. I'm new in town. . ." There are a hundred variations, but it really doesn't matter exactly what you say; the other person will probably have a feeling about you after the third word. If you see a negative reaction you can back down by interrupting yourself with, "I can see I am intruding, if you change your mind and would like to talk just say 'hi'." This is actually one of the best things you can do, since it shows that you are sensitive and will not impose your will on other people. You just might hear a "hi" as you walk away or a few minutes later if your paths cross again. I have. Remember that attitude is everything. If you are truly concerned that you don't offend the other person, and make it clear that you will not be insistent, you will stand the best chance of making a friend. Be ready and willing to accept rejection gracefully. Persistence rarely pays off with a stranger.

A joke can turn rejection into a pleasant experience, "I can see you don't want to talk, but let me tell you this joke so I can leave you smiling." Select a clean, short joke. For example, a friend of mine just came up with the true definition of reality: the annoying time between naps. Another quick joke is: Did you hear in the news about the suicidal, dyslexic twin, who killed her sister by mistake. If upon approaching someone and they say, "I don't speak to strangers." You can still salvage the moment with, "Then just allow me to ask you a question that requires no reply: Why do they put Braille dots on the keypad of the drive up ATM?" Smile and walk away or try, "If you change your mind and would like to talk, just say 'hi'."

People you meet in the above manner usually assume that you are looking for a romance. If this is not the case (remember, you were looking for friends) make your intentions known during this first talk. Of course you still have to be careful. If you want to maintain a platonic relationship, you must avoid sex like the plague. Sex changes everything. One way to do this is to draw a solid line at kissing. No kissing. After knowing the person for a while, you can experience the feeling of human warmth through loving touches and embraces safe from the danger of sex changing everything. Kissing always leads to sex. If you can keep sex out the relationships you know should be platonic. You could be friends forever.

The Friendship Force

Or Strange Idea #30

One of my favorite stories is how Bonnie and Roi met. Bonnie was over in Germany working as a teacher. One weekend she decided to help pick grapes at a local vineyard. If you pick grapes, they give you some of the wine you helped to make. While she was picking she met an American engineer, Roi. They started talking and it came out that she had spent a year in Okinawa. When Roi heard "Okinawa", he jokingly said, "Then you must have met my old buddy, Paul Winter." In shock, Bonnie responded, "Not only did we meet, but I just got a letter from him".

There seems to be some force that favors people who value friendships, and it helps them remain close to their friends.

I remember how I lost Dave Walker. Dave and I had been through a harrowing experience in the Alps, the kind that brings men together, but fate intervened.

When I lived in Germany and wanted to go skiing, I would sometimes stay at a hotel where Dave lived. He was an American climbing guide and ski instructor/patrol liaison. He liked to ski Kitzbuhel so he tried to get his day off to correspond with my visit. I always skied Kitzbuhel so we skied together. Dave was the best skier I had ever seen and I, having been a ski instructor at the age of 16, was no slouch. Often when I skied people would cheer. I liked rugged terrain skiing and could rarely find anyone willing to ski with me. In the seventies few people skied off the packed slopes, but the steep and deep was what Dave and I lived for.

For miles around people could see us bounding down cliff areas near the tops of the mountains. I am sure that any American who saw us must have thought, God, these Europeans can ski.

One late afternoon found us near the bottom of the valley but miles away from the town where I had parked my car. Dave wanted to take the bus but I convinced him that we could go up one more time and just traverse the lower portion of the Hahnenkamm.

After much climbing around ravines and very little traversing we found ourselves skiing in the dark with sparks visibly shooting from our skis because we couldn't see the rock encrusted bare spots. We were hungry but all we had was a small piece of chocolate which served as our dinner. We finally came to the bottom of a chair lift that started part way up the mountain and went to the very top. The lift structure had a map on its side, but the sky was overcast, making it completely dark. I took off my skis and got on Dave's shoulders so I could get close enough to read it.

The map was ten feet wide but, unbelievably, the town where I had parked my car was not even on the map. What made matters worse was that the map indicated we were at a dead end. The only way out without skiing through the trees was the lift, which would not start again until the morning. Skiing through the trees is something Dave and I both love, but the Austrians graze their cattle on the lower parts of the mountains during the summer, so you have to keep an eye out for barbed wire fences. To ski through woods on an overcast night was madness if only because branches were so hard to see. Throw in the barbed wire fences and it would take a miracle to come through unscathed.

Unfortunately we had no choice. We couldn't wait until morning because we were both dressed in light clothes so we could ski hard without getting overheated. Also, I had come down with my friend Maria, and had told her that we would be back at my car around 4:00.

We entered the woods at 5:30 and started skiing. The dips and bumps were undetectable and I would sometimes find my knees in my face or my stomach in my throat, but neither Dave nor I fell. Suddenly the miracle happened. Dave pulled an instantaneous stop and stared at his boots. I stopped behind him. Four inches above the snow and just in front his skis was a single line of barbed wire. His ski would have gone under it and he would have experienced a fall I doubt he may not have skied away from. To this day I find it hard to believe that he was able to see that little piece of wire. He was amazing.

Soon after the wire incident we came upon salvation: a logging road. All we had to do was ski down the nice, smooth, gently sloping logging road to the main road and hitch a ride. Dave went first, I followed. Suddenly he disappeared. One moment he was there, then he vanished. I kept skiing and noticed a black spot in the road. When I stopped and looked at it, it looked back. It was Dave. He was in a large hole right in the middle of the road. He was having trouble getting his skis free. When we got him out, his skis were OK, thank God. That was pretty lucky. When you run a pair of skis into the side of a hole that you are not prepared for, breaking a tip is a common result.

We started out again with Dave still in the lead. At one point I noticed that the road curved for no apparent reason. I decided to cut the corner. As I skied off the road, the unpacked snow felt heavenly under my skis – but it didn't last. Suddenly I was falling. I had skied right off a cliff. Below was a pile of rocks made by the same river that had cut the cliff. I spun around in the air and grabbed for the wall of the cliff. The unpacked snow I had gone through had slowed me down or I would have traveled too far out. I managed to get a hold of the cliff wall after falling only a few feet and glued myself to it. I hung there trying to imitate a suction cup while I yelled my head off for Dave. I thought that any move would cause me to fall off the wall, and it was only a matter of time before I would lose my grip. It had been years since I had done any climbing and I had lost the "feel" that lets you know when you have a good grip and when you are about to slip. Not to mention that climbing rock with skis on is impossible. I hoped Dave would hear me and come back before it was too late.

Dave can be incredibly calm sometimes. His head appeared over the edge of the cliff. Looking down at me, clinging for dear life, he smiled and said, "Just traversing, Paul?"

I was talking very quietly now, afraid that one more yell and I would slip, " Dave, old buddy, give me your pole. Just be a real nice guy and give me your pole."

"I don't know, Paul, I think these are those newfangled poles where the handle comes off if you catch the other end in a bush or something. Let me just pull on it a while to make sure it doesn't come off."

"Daaaaaaaaaaaaave!"

Now I realized that Dave was an expert climber and had assessed the situation and realized that I was not going to slip at all. He was just getting back at me because, after all, this was all my fault. He finally reached down with his pole and pulled me up. I noticed my life had become a little more precious to me.

We skied down to the road without further incident. The first car picked us up and we had a surprisingly warm reunion with Maria, despite being three hours late. She said that she would have been frantic if I had been alone, but since Dave was with me she thought we would eventually make it back. Dave just smiled and said not one word about traversing.

When my work was over and it was time to leave Europe, I took a couple of months off for a final drive around the Old World. One of my stops was Dave's hotel because I wanted to get his stateside address. They told me he had left months ago and they didn't have a forwarding address. I was depressed, I really liked him a lot. He was an amazing, sensitive, considerate guy. One of a kind.

Five years later I was still living overseas but I had finally become tired of being a foreigner wherever I left my house. It was time to go back to the states and settle down. I flew to the Lake Tahoe area with a friend to check out the skiing since I was considering the San Francisco Bay area to settle down in. We found a motel that had kitchenettes, then went to the supermarket. I was walking through the produce section going back to my friend. I had an avocado in each hand and visions of guacamole in my head when a man walked by me and nodded. I nodded back because he looked familiar, but then I remembered that I lived in Japan. How could I know anybody around here? Unless they were a long lost friend. After a moment it came to me whom he looked like. I said to my friend, "Remember that story I told you, about being lost in the Alps? That guy over there looks just like..." I turned and pointed in his direction and saw that he was pointing me out to a woman who looked like the singer at the hotel where we met so many years before. I remembered her clearly because both our instruments of choice were left handed 12-string guitars. You don't find many of them around and she was pretty special too.

Eight thousand miles from our fateful traverse, our paths had crossed once again. The chances of that happening are astronomically small. It wasn't luck, it was the friendship force. This is why I have told you this story. There seems to be a force that brings lost friends together *if* you work at maintaining the friends you have. I was being rewarded for all the times I struggled to get out the pen or the phone and keep in touch with my friends. Friends must be very important to whatever makes things happen. Make them important to you and you will be repaid a thousand times over.

Respect and Lovers

A healthy intimate relationship helps maintain peace of mind, but such relationships are often elusive. At lest there is one clear indicator of trouble. Loss of respect for one's partner signals an immediate need for attention. Of course, avoiding loss of respect is much easier than trying to recover from it. To prevent losing respect, you need a balanced level of communication. Not too much and definitely not too little. Intuition can help you decide on how much, but you must at least consider communicating about every behavior or incident that you perceive as being thoughtless, inconsiderate, or unkind. Sometimes, it only requires asking why. Sometimes, your partner is hoping you would ask why.

A person is not always aware that their behavior is objectionable. What appears to be a transgression to you may have been common practice in your lover's family. This or some other information can completely change your perspective on an incident. If the act was unquestionably offensive, a lot of communication and a sincere determination to prevent a reoccurrence may be needed. Sometimes change is needed, but even before change takes place, you will feel immensely better from simply talking it out. You will experience real emotional bonding. You may even have a bonus of that wonderful physical bonding we all enjoy so much. This bonding is a hell of a lot of fun and is even more wonderful after a tense discussion. Plus, your relationship will become more secure because each time you communicate successfully it becomes easier to do so.

Successful communication often relies on resisting the temptation to become defensive. There is always an excuse for being thoughtless. There is an excuse for everything. Therefore, excuses don't mean anything and they usually make the problem worse. Excuses and explanations make you appear insincere and despicable. It doesn't matter if you were stressed out, tired or in a hurry. You will be all of those things again. Does that allow you to be thoughtless again? The urge to become defensive is tremendous. Recognize it and respond to your mate's attempt at communication with appreciation. Acknowledge your thoughtless act as simply that and try saying something like: "I could have treated you better; you surely deserve it."

Recognize that it often takes a lot of courage for your lover to bring up an issue. Assume that the motivation to do so is based on a desire to stay together and have a good relationship. Do not assume that it is based on a desire to get back at you, even if it appears that way to you. This is an old defense mechanism that we play on ourselves. It comes from fear of being in the wrong. This fear also brings on anger, a reaction that needs to be recognized quickly. Assume that your mate's motivation is based on the love and respect that they have for you, and be willing to accept at least half the responsibility for the way you have made them feel. Realize that the discussion of issues is the only way to maintain respect and that your lover is trying to maintain the respect they have for you. Resist the temptation to avoid issues in the name of a smooth sailing relationship. Such relationships die a slow, quiet, certain death.

An issue left unexplored will soon be forgotten, but the damage will have a permanent effect on the way you feel about your lover. The great tragedy is that you will soon get used to this small drop in the respect you had for them. Numerous loses of respect like this, over a long period of time, can go unnoticed. Then, one day, you will suddenly realize that you no longer respect your lover. At that point your relationship is doomed unless you can rebuild the respect. Communicating is a real challenge, but compared to rebuilding respect, communication is a breeze.

Unfortunately, it can be difficult just to find the right moment to communicate a problem. It is easy to let the issue slip away, forgotten, but not without damage to the relationship. One beautiful way to avoid this problem is to set aside a special flower vase for the purpose of communication. Whenever you need to talk about an issue, put a flower in the vase. One flower for each issue. This way you will not forget that you have something to talk about. Don't identify the problem before hand. Let your mate's curiosity add incentive to find the time. Resist the temptation to talk about it when there is not enough time for a real talk. Try to use a real flower, but keep dried flowers handy. A real flower will reflect your situation better because you can see the flower wilt as the damage to your relationship slowly occurs. If a dried flower gets dusty, you know you are in big trouble. May your vase never hold a wilted or dusty flower.

5 – Special Tools

By now you may suspect that worry (negative visualization) will adversely affect your well-being and impede your progress towards peace of mind. Unfortunately, worry as well as the elimination of worry take a while to demonstrate their effects. However, there are some tools that have immediate effect for which it helps to maintain an open-mind with these tools. Although it is not essential, consider temporarily putting aside any need you have for proof and for just a few moments, adopt the attitude that a skeptic is simply someone who has fewer tools to make things happen. With that consideration in mind, jump into the first two special tools:

- Present Time – this tool can increase the intensity of even the slightest pleasure
- Center of Mind – this tool can improve your mental sharpness especially affecting understanding of complex concepts and verbal acumen.

The Present Time Tool

It is not intelligence that allows us to hear our intuitive messages, but rather quietness of mind. A person who lives a simpler life is more likely to have that quiet mind. If someone's life is full of responsibilities and activities, their mind can be too involved with future actions and past problems to notice relatively minor changes in the way they feel.

The modern world has so many opportunities. It would border on the criminal to lead a simple life in the midst of such opportunity. There are libraries where computers can search any subject in seconds, musical instrument systems that will write the sheet music as you play, free lectures and concerts, and inexpensive classes where you can learn anything from acrobatics to zoology. If you have any ambition to

114

improve yourself and experience a richer life, you can spend every waking moment increasing your knowledge and skills at almost no cost.

People who appreciate these opportunities often work, attend classes, and participate in sports or dance.... These are the people who could most benefit from using intuition because making decisions with intuition eliminates a lot of the time-consuming aspects of decision-making. Unfortunately, because of all the things these people have on their minds, using intuition may be very difficult. In the beginning, what they need most is to quiet their busy minds.

The first step is to stop thinking about the past *and* the future. The most effective way to do this is to view the task at hand with fascination. This is the essence of "Present Time." Although this is more difficult than it sounds, anybody can learn it. All that is needed is motivation and a bit of practice. Motivation will come from the knowledge that Present Time increases the pleasure of many activities. When you reach the point where you can do it while engaged in fairly complicated tasks, you can then use Present Time to improve your performance as well. The only way to get good at it is to use it often, at least three times a day. This will give you the skill to be in Present Time while accessing your intuition. The good news is that you will not have to interrupt your schedule in the slightest way at all in order to practice Present Time.

There are many opportunities during the day when your mind is free to wander: when you drive, when you walk, when you wait for the copy machine. In line at a store you often have way too much of this time. During these moments most people are thinking about past events, projecting into future ones, wondering: Did I turn off the gas? Do my socks match? These thoughts prevent you from being aware of the present and move you away from really experiencing how you feel. In order to be sensitive to your intuition you must be in close contact with your present feelings. This can only be accomplished by learning how to, at least temporarily, leave past events in the past and refrain from thinking of the future. Become aware of your feelings *now*. The best time to do that is whenever you are doing something that you want to last a long time or that feels so good you want to heighten the sensation. Unfortunately, you must learn how to get into Present Time while performing other activities. For that you need a little practice.

Present Time Practice

You can practice Present Time whenever your mind is free to wander:

1. Rotate your shoulders forward, up, back and down, one at a time. Relax and breathe deeply.
2. Stop thinking about things you have done or things you want to do.
3. Observe your surroundings with wonder, as if you have never seen them before, imagine you are a baby seeing the shape, size, and color of the things around you for the first time. The key word to Present Time is wonder. Look at things with wonder.

Regain the joy of discovering simple things by looking at them as if it were the first time you had ever seen them. You can accomplish this because it has been a long time since you looked at everyday things in this manner. You can have the joy of a baby again. The following are suggested times to do this:

Walking Down Halls

Select a favorite place that you walk by every day and reserve it for Present Time, but don't limit yourself to these places. Notice the texture of the wall, feel the air like a liquid as you walk through it, feel its coolness as it flows into your throat. Feel the handle of a door. Feel how hard the metal is but how smooth.

Driving

Since you spend so much time driving it may not be possible to perform all your driving in Present Time although it is the safest way to drive. At least select a five minute section of the most attractive part of your daily drive and reserve it for Present Time driving. Turn off the radio. Look at the greenery on the side of the road. Look at the clouds in the sky. Feel the vibrations of the car, let it relax your body but excite your mind. If you are about to shift, get involved. Feel the pedals with your feet, listen to the engine, and notice the tachometer out of the bottom of your eye as you look straight ahead out the windshield. Happy trails.

In Line At The Stores

Ignore the conversations you can clearly hear and listen to the murmur of the voices in the background – like soft fabric pushed into your ear. See and hear the things around you as a baby would: with wonder.

Eating

Have you ever thought about an engrossing subject while eating one of your favorite foods and suddenly the food is all gone but you hardly noticed it? Eating as a baby, as if it were the first time you ever experienced this flavor, not only prevents this from happening but makes the flavor of the food more intense. When you eat in Present Time you will savor every mouthful. To help you stay in Present Time, concentrate on recognizing each of the different flavors that most dishes have. When you recognize one, search for another. It will help if you close your eyes. People subconsciously close their eyes when they taste something exceptional to intensify the flavor. Frequently, after a good chew, swallow everything in your mouth *completely*. This allows you to enjoy the after taste of the food and makes the meal last a lot longer. Some foods, like chocolate, have a wonderful after-taste which can last a long time. When you eat in Present Time you will realize that on the list of Present Time activities the best was saved for last.

Visit Present Time until you become aware of a change in the way you feel when you get there. Eventually you will be able to make yourself feel this way and you will automatically be in Present Time. Once you have reached this point you are ready to use Present Time to help you excel at any task you choose. Simply get the Present Time feeling when you want to increase the intensity of a pleasure or improve the outcome of the a task. Remember to view the task with fascination and wonder. If you would like to increase your motivation to practice Present Time, realize that performing it while executing a simple task is actually an effective and easy meditation. So now, you can meditate while cleaning the house, folding laundry... and give some meaning to drudgery. Present Time is a powerful state of mind from which you can very effectively access your intuition if there is nothing at a deeper level blocking your way.

Center of Mind

After I stopped traveling for Hughes Aircraft, I became a systems engineer. After a couple of years on the job, I began to have trouble following technical conversations. Although I was in my thirties I actually thought that the mental sharpness of youth was fading. Then, I learned a new approach for viewing human awareness. It proposes that awareness has physical mobility. That is, our center of awareness is able to move about and around our body. More significantly: a person is able to obtain heightened use of their faculties by gathering this center of awareness into oneself.

The method for getting this heightened use of your faculties is called Center of Mind. It is a simple visualization that can be maintained while performing most any other operation. The first time I tried to use this method it was during a conversation: I noticed that I could follow the conversation more easily. Full of hope, I went home thinking I might have found the solution to my problem with technical conversations.

Although the visualization was not complicated, I soon realized that I would have to practice it for a while before I could do it whenever I wanted. This was one practice that would come easy since I enjoyed the feeling of heightened senses that resulted from it. After a week, I had greatly improved my ability to do the visualization while performing others tasks, even if they were quite complicated. This ability turned out to be extremely important.

When I had developed confidence in my ability to hold this visualization while I did other things, I knew I was ready to talk to the engineer at work whom I called "The Brain". When the time came I was very excited. If it was going to work, "The Brain" would be the acid test. He started talking, I did Center of Mind and listened. At first I didn't notice anything, but then I realized that I remembered and understood everything that he said. I was ecstatic. That night I celebrated; I had Center of Mind:

1. Take a depth breath and relax.

2. Get into Present Time.
3. Image that you are a very small replica of yourself and that you are sitting inside your own head looking out through portholes that are your eyes.

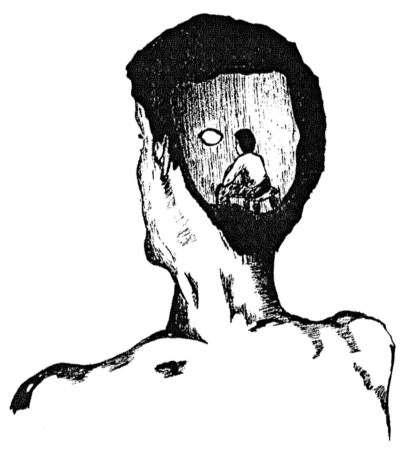

Figure 2. Center Of Mind

In A Tutu

I was once in a meeting that was lead by a powerful headstrong engineering manager. He was brilliant, but his interpersonal style was so intimidating that I secretly bestowed a title on him: The Intimidator. Once, we were reviewing the design of an electronic system for a new jet aircraft. This system had to work at high temperatures. The Intimidator thought we were making the system cost too much because we were overcompensating for the thermal environment. He was technically very sharp and decided to go over the design in detail. He started asking, "Why did you do it that way?" every ten seconds or so.

When there are many functions to design, the decision to do something a certain way isn't always documented. Later on it is often hard to remember, especially in a meeting with The Intimidator, why you did something a certain way. When he was cross-examining one of the engineers who couldn't remember some details of a circuit he had designed, The Intimidator decided that we would go through the entire design process from the start. The engineer must have thought that The Intimidator had found a big mistake and was about to make him look like a fool. This engineer got so rattled when we started redesigning the circuit that he forgot the most basic principle of electrical engineering: Ohms law. ($V = IR$ or voltage equals current times resistance.) I thought to myself that nobody will ever be able to intimidate me like that.

Wrong.

Two weeks later I stood in front of The Intimidator with a completely blank mind as he asked me questions concerning an analysis I had recently written. I couldn't think at all and knew that I looked like a complete idiot. I couldn't believe that The Intimidator had done to me what I had sworn would never happen. I was terrified and it turned out that I had no reason to be. I had not made a mistake, but simply could not remember why I had used one number instead of another. It was nothing but fear that had emptied my mind. Later I felt helpless because I thought he could do that to me at anytime. I had to find a solution.

Our attitude has a great effect on our luck, a good attitude makes good luck. I must have had a great attitude at that time because a few weeks after my first encounter with The Intimidator, I learned about "getting people out of my space". The premise is that another person's energy can interfere with the area or "space" you use for thinking. I wasn't sure if I believed all this talk about a energy and space, but the Intimidator was clearly interfering with the way people normally thought. The rest of the premise is that you can move a person out of your space by making an embarrassing image of them in your mind. If it is a man, you can picture them in a tutu. When I first learned of this I didn't think it could possibly work, but it appealed to my sense of humor, and I didn't have any better ideas

Less than a week later I got my chance. The Intimidator was reviewing another analysis I had written. He was doing it right in the hall by the secretary's desk. If he started finding mistakes it was going to be really embarrassing. He started in by magically finding the one area in the analysis that I was not sure of. When he asked me about it I didn't know what to say. Then I remembered the tutu. I made a picture of him in my mind. He had on a woman's ballet outfit, see the next page, and boy did he look embarrassed. I couldn't help but smile, and suddenly I had all the time in the world to formulate a good reply. It worked. I remembered all the details of that section and even came up with a new justification for the numbers I used. After the review, I wondered if the tutu would help in all confrontational situations. It did.

Try the Tutu combined with Center of Mind whenever you get into a confrontational situation. You may notice that you stop suffering from "delayed eloquence". You will no longer think of clever things to say five minutes after the encounter. You will think of them during the encounter.

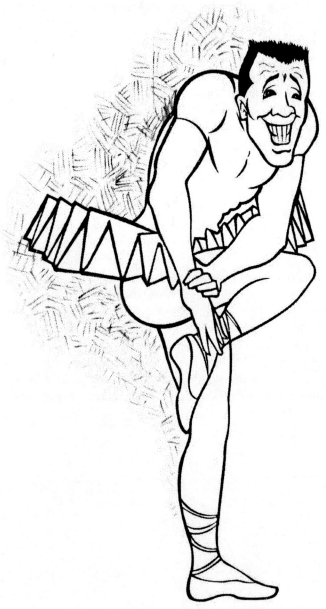

Figure 3. Put Him in a Tutu.

122

Of course it is not always a man that is The Intimidator, so here is a little fun for that woman Intimidator. Picture the woman Intimidator in front of a meeting saying, "This whole project is falling apart!" Just then she drops her papers, bends down to pick it up, and splits her skirt.

Figure 4. ". . . this whole project is falling apart."

Amusement

No instruction on the subject of improving your mental faculties would be complete without a few words about amusement. These words will be in the form of a story about Fast Eddy, a man for whom I once had the pleasure to work.

Ed called a meeting of his people consisting of about 20 technical types and some support staff. There were a number of new folks in our group, so Ed asked that we go around the table, say our name, and talk about what we do. When it was my turn I said my name and defied Ed by stating that I didn't like anybody to know what I did. I meant it to be funny, but it was too close to the truth and made Ed look like a boss whose people didn't follow his ideas. This was a bad precedent to set, considering the new folks at the meeting. Ed looked at me with surprise, laughed, and told everybody that I did operational and front end analysis, made sure things ran well in the lab, and that I would be straightening things up in the lab over the next few days. The lab was an incredibly dirty mess since it was a special security area and the regular cleaning people could not get into it. Ed had seen a need to put me in my place and in two seconds had found a constructive way to do it. I didn't feel vengeful since I knew I deserved it (yes I have learned self-responsibility). Everybody else was happy that someone was finally going to clean up the lab, and glad it wasn't them.

I noticed after that fateful meeting that whenever I took a problem to Fast Eddy he always did the same thing. He made a moderate chuckle, and then gave me an enlightened solution. I wanted to know how he came up with such good solutions so quickly, but didn't pay much attention to the chuckle; I just thought he was a jolly fellow. Finally, after analyzing a number of our conversations, I realized what he was doing when he was searching for a solution, he was laughing.

I started to use his tool. It worked superbly. I have since discovered that not only is amusement the best state of mind for quickly solving problems, but when you laugh, people think that you have found a great solution and they start matching the feeling of finding a solution. Even if no solutions come into your own head, you have put everybody else in the right state of mind to find the solution on their own.

Remember use it, don't prove it.

At first I thought that I could not laugh without having something to laugh about, but I soon learned differently. It was actually quite easy to make the sound of laughter whenever I wanted to. Directly after I do this, it seems so silly that I gave out a genuine laugh. With just a little practice you, too, can laugh on command, but you do need to practice before you do it in a problem situation when there are other people around. This is how you do it: laugh. Just make the sound. You can imitate the laugh of someone whose laugh you like or just imitate your own laugh. I think the best laugh to go for is a deep, soft, knowing kind of laugh, as opposed to a "crack up" laugh. You don't have to feel funny, but you do have to let go of something. I think that you will find that once you make the sound of a laugh you will follow it with a real laugh.

The letting go of "something" when you laugh seems to be the essence of the problem solving state of mind that amusement produces, but I have yet to put a finger on what that something is. This is typical of my attitude for getting along in the world: if it works, use it. However, if you have a lot of time on your hands, maybe, you can figure out why it works.

Now would be a good time for you to practice your laugh on command. It helps a little if nobody is around, but if there is somebody there they will just think you read something funny in this book. If they ask what is so funny, ask them whether they thought your laugh was forced or natural. You will most likely find that when you laugh on command nobody will think you are imitating the sound of laughter; they will just think that you thought of something funny. When you learn to laugh on command you will be able to create for yourself a positive and effective attitude for solving problems quickly. Laughing on command is also good for helping you find that elusive word that is right on the tip of your tongue.

This laughing tool has another application: presentations. You can use this laugh when you are in front of a group of people and you get tongue-tied. I do not mean when you are dealing with an Intimidator. I am referring to moments when you have done it to yourself with your own fear. A couple of examples: someone asks you a question and you think you should know the answer but you don't, or suddenly you see a giant hole in your own argument as you are talking. This last cause of fear has happened to me a couple of times and I later realized that the "hole" that had gotten me so flustered was actually never there. My own fear tied me up.

The laugh on command can save you whenever you have reduced your ability to operate due to fear. When you feel there is no time to think, the laugh seems to create a natural pause during which you will find tremendous time. Don't worry, you can laugh for no apparent reason and people will not think you have lost your mind. If you laugh with a knowing smile, it makes everybody think that you know something that they don't. If you are dealing with adversaries they might think that it is something embarrassing about them. This may unnerve them. Whatever the case, once you start speaking you don't have to relate anything funny. Your adversaries will be thankful that you decided to spare them from some embarrassing story and your supporters will be glad that you found your pace again.

This laugh on command will also work when you are having problems in a one-on-one discussion or in discussions of any size as long as there are no intimidators operating in your space. The effect of the laugh can be beaten by an intimidator. Get the intimidator out of your space first, then, use the laugh. If you use the tutu image you will have something to laugh about and everything will fall into place very nicely. These tools, combined with Center of Mind, can give you the control and confidence to use your mind to the full extent of its ability in any circumstance.

With these tools you may begin to embrace problems. You may actually take on a personality trait that many engineers fall victim to. This personality trait is beautifully demonstrated in a very old story from the French revolution. This engineer (engineers have been around since the pyramids) was to be executed along with a farmer and a priest for protecting some royalty from the rioting mobs. The thing that makes the story interesting is a little known rule about the guillotine. If the guillotine fails to work after the blade has dropped, the prisoner is set free. The priest went first. The blade was released and went sliding down the greased tracks Suddenly it came to a screeching halt just inches from the priest's neck . He was set free; a very happy priest and no further a friend of royalty. The same thing happened to the farmer, but as the engineer was lead up to the guillotine he exclaimed, "I see your problem."

Sometimes, it is better to let someone else find the solution.

Spiritual Considerations

A spiritual explanation for the tools in this chapter, is presented here for your consideration. It is not presented in order to prove the validity of these tools or the validity of spiritual beliefs. Also, no spiritual belief is necessary for using these tools or your intuition. These explanations are supplied merely as possible answers for the person who asks, why or how do these tools work.

The spiritual concepts which best yield an explanation for the effectiveness of the tools are as follows:

1. The spirit and body are two separate entities loosely bound together.
2. The spirit has some mobility outside the body and can expand to fill up great spaces and perhaps transcend space.
3. Emotional problems can damage the spirit.
4. A damaged spirit can cause health problems for the body.

As a simplified definition, the spirit can be identified as an intelligent part of a person that has a will of its own. The body may not be consciously aware of the will of the spirit. The body operates on a more animal level and is usually concerned with things like survival, power, and sex. Another way to think of the spirit is as "personal energy" that has intelligence and which operates within the realm of the subconscious.

When personal energy is diffused and not centered close to the body a person does not have optimal use of their faculties. Personal energy may move away from the center of the body for a number of reasons:

If the Body is in Pain

The awareness of pain is reduced when personal energy moves away from the body. This may be one of the reasons why it is often difficult to think clearly when you are in pain. However, truly effective pain control can only be obtained by moving back into your body and exercising control over the pain mechanisms.

To Gain Control

By moving your personal energy into the space of another person, you can increase your control over that person. People who do this regularly give others headaches.

To More Closely Observe

In a mistaken attempt to gain more information about a person or thing, your personal energy can move into that space. The problem with this is that you then no longer have full use of your faculties with which to observe. Things will not be as vibrant and details may elude you. Plus you are likely to lose the cooperation of the other person when they begin to feel invaded.

When someone is intent on making a point, their personal energy can move right into the space where you do your thinking and reasoning. When someone else's personal energy is in your thinking and reasoning space it can become confusing and difficult to think clearly. This is why it is hard to think when faced with an intimidator.

The following experiment suggests the possibility that you can affect a person without using direct methods such as speech, and that perhaps there is something operating between people that cannot be detected by the five senses. Could this be personal energy?

The Eye Experiment

The next time you are out in public, find someone who is standing in a place where no one is likely to stare at them, for example, in the aisles at the supermarket or in line at the bank. It is important that you not be in their line of sight or even in their peripheral vision. Start to stare at that person. Usually that person will turn in your direction for no apparent reason, unless they are absorbed in some engrossing mental process of their own. Try this with five or six people.

Perhaps you have already noticed this phenomenon but find it hard to connect it to personal energy. However, you will probably acknowledge that somehow you are affecting the person who looks up. When that person is engaged in his or her own space; he or she is not sending anything over to monitor you. It is reasonable to assume, then, that something from you is getting over there and making itself known to him or her. What do you want to call it?

Faith in Intuition

You may often hear, "You have to believe in it or it will not work". This idea addresses a real problem, but is missing the point. The following story may clear it up:

Some boys are standing around, talking about the Olympic gymnastics events on TV the previous night. Suddenly the smallest boy says, "I can do a handstand." Nobody believes him, and in their minds they are seeing him fall and land in some comical way. A grin spreads through the group. The little guy says, "oh yeah? I'll show you." Everybody in the group has been visualizing him fall. When he tries his handstand, of course he falls. "I did it last night!", he exclaims. He did, but there wasn't a bunch of negative visualizers standing around.

When you say you don't believe in something you are often visualizing the outcome you expect. People who are about to perform some difficult action often worry about their own failure. In other words, they negatively visualize their failure, and thereby ensure it. You don't need to be a believer in intuition, but you must take care not to be a negative visualizer.

Soon you will learn how to use your intuition. Therefore, it is time to warn you about losing it. You cannot give it away, but it can be taken from you by negative visualization, and by something else: ego. If you tell people about your new-found ability, your fear of failure combined with their negativity and jealousy can rob you of your new ability. If you really want to share the benefits that you receive from this book with your friends, simply give them a copy and tell them that it worked for you. Don't tell them what worked; just tell them that they must find out for themselves. Resist being the teacher; people are more likely to try something they read than something someone tells them. If you try to teach them, their competitive nature may cause them to prove to you that it is all self-fulfilling prophecy or some other scientific negativity.

Do not use the intuition technique when someone asks, "What does that intuition stuff tell you?", unless you are sure they value your intuition and are not testing you. Never use your intuition to prove to someone that it works. Your own fear of failing in front of someone is likely to interfere. A person must make the investment and experience the exploration for themselves if they want to truly know the value of intuition.

Environment

Or Strange Idea #31

Have you ever seen a painting and said to yourself, "That's beautiful"? Of course you have, but what is it about a painting that makes you think it is beautiful? Do you think to yourself, "this painting has good balance and the artist has used my favorite colors"? Of course not. The first thing you think is, that's beautiful. Right away. Then, a few seconds later, you might analyze why you feel that way. The way you feel is the key.

What you see affects the way you feel. One of the rewards of becoming more aware of your deeper feelings as you search for peace of mind is an increased sensitivity to your environment. Of course, this is a disadvantage if you have to walk through the streets of The South Bronx everyday. But, if you have some control over your environment and want to feel good without using distractions, you can put your environment to work for you. By making simple changes to your surroundings you can greatly improve their effect on you. This may soon become more important because your sensitivity to environment increases as you become more aware of your deeper feelings in order to access your intuition. One indication that you are not in close touch with your feelings is having a messy home and an unpleasant work space and not noticing it's bad effect on how you feel.

One of the most significant and least developed environments is your work place. Most people spend more waking hours at their desk than anywhere else. If you want to feel better more often, carefully construct your visual environment where you spend the most time – your office. If you do it right, people will comment on how nice it looks. What they will actually be reacting to is how good your office makes them feel. Be careful, the people who don't consciously associate the good feeling that your office gives them to the way it looks may subconsciously relate the good feeling to visiting you and you will never get rid of them.

If you want to have your office environment positively influence how you feel, the key is to create as natural an environment as possible. Here are a few suggestions:

Nature in your field of view

Even when your head is down to read something on your desk you can work some natural scene into your field of view. Find posters of natural scenes with the horizon near the bottom of the poster. This will make your office look and feel bigger and more "outdoors". If your desk is up against a wall, hang the poster so low that its bottom is at desk top level. Decorators always say the center of a painting should be at eye level. So having a poster start at the top of your desk is close to the norm because you are sitting down 99% of the time. Decorate to make your office feel the best from a sitting down position at your desk, not a standing position.

Eliminate Straight Lines

Straight lines are unnatural and never feel as good as the forms of nature. The most effective way to eliminate straight lines is to put plants in the corners of the office. Avoid posters of cities or abstract art that contains straight lines. Place a plant next to your computer and have it grow around the straight border of the monitor to break this straight line that is constantly in your field of view.

Amplify the Available Natural Scenes

Most homes have natural scenes right outside the window. Increase their good effect. Block as little of the windows as possible. Buy long curtain rods so that none of the window is blocked when the curtains are drawn back. If you like curtain arrangements, place them on the blank wall alongside the window. If the scene outside is unpleasant, move. You can't realize how bad your surroundings are making you feel if you are always in a bad environment. People who live in ugly cities have often told me that they get used to how ugly it looks. It's true, people get used to feeling bad.

Use Lots of Plants

Place plants just to the side of the window. Not only will this frame the natural scene outside, but also it will effectively bring it closer and eliminate the straight line of the window edge. Don't hang plants in front of windows. This blocks the natural scene outside and makes it appear further away. Use plants to break up straight lines of corners. This way the plants will grow towards you.

Put the Out-of-doors in Your Field-of-view

Arrange furniture based on what you see when you sit down and whenever possible make that a natural scene. Many people arrange furniture to look good when you first walk into the room. You only spend 5 seconds walking into the room but hours sitting in the chairs. The chair you spend the most time in should face the out-of-doors. Arrange the less used, conversational chair/couch grouping more towards the interior of the room.

The Grounding Tool

Another powerful visualization is grounding. Grounding will increase your ability to obtain and stay in the Center of Mind. It is also used in removing blocks, and is the tool that will remove the discomfort that can arise when a person starts to come into contact with blocks that result from emotionally painful issues. This visualization is widely recognized and can be found in many different meditations. Some of its other uses include reducing anxiety and increasing control of your concentration in meditations, and control over the flow of different energies that run through your body (the same energy flow on which acupuncture is based).

Grounding can be a little complicated at first, so it helps to practice at a time when you will be able to relax and in an environment where there are no distractions. After you have practiced once a day for a couple of weeks you should be able to ground on command even in a stressful situation. Although it may seem like a difficult tool at first, the practice of it can be a valuable break from the hustle and bustle that starts for many people the moment they get out of bed.

How to Ground:

1. Select a time and location where you will be able to relax without distractions.
2. Find a chair that will allow you to sit straight with both feet flat on the floor.
3. Get into Present Time.
4. Take a few deep breaths, rotate your shoulders forward, up, back and down, one at a time.
5. Relax your whole body but keep your shoulders back. Close your eyes.
6. Get into Center of Mind.
7. From your vantage point in the center of your head, picture your body below you.
8. Add to this picture of your body a long object that is attached to the base of your spine. Imagine that this object develops downward through the floor and attaches to the center of the Earth.

This object is your grounding cord. It can be made of any material you wish. One of the most popular grounding cords is a tree trunk that ends in a strong root system at the center of the Earth, but it can be a pipe, an anchor chain, or anything you like. When you ground, avoid effort. Simply be aware of your grounding cord, look at it with wonder, and stay in the center of your head.

Practice grounding for two or three minutes a day and whenever you need a little help to stay in Center of Mind. You will find that grounding helps keep you in Center of Mind and vice versa. If you can maintain this picture and prevent the usual thoughts that walk through your mind, you have learned a meditation. The longer you quiet your thoughts, stay in Present Time, and remain grounded and centered, the more peaceful and calm you will feel during the rest of the day and you will think and listen more clearly. It is normal for your mind to resist being "empty" and to want to follow thoughts, so do not be disappointed at first. Simply let your mind follow the thought for a moment then gently return to being aware of your grounding cord from the center of your head.

The Multiple Universe Tool

I use this tool to make things work out the way I would love. This tool is the reason for my reply when people ask me if I can predict the future. My reply:

> You can't predict the future, there are too many of them. It is by far better to control the future. Or more accurately control which future you will go to.

A few days after I discovered the Multiple Universe tool, I read an article in Newsweek magazine about a Harvard physicist who was convinced that many parallel universes must exist due to evidence of the existence of much more mass that can be explained by our known universe. One thing was sure, I was convinced that multiple universes did indeed exist because this tool worked. It was however nice of Newsweek to supply that verification.

The Multiple Universe Visualization
1. Close your eyes.
2. Imagine that the thing you would love to see occur has already occurred and that you are reflecting on this wonderful occurrence.
3. Embrace and explore that feeling so you can recover it in easily.
4. Clear your mind of this image and quiet your thoughts. Breath deeply. Relax.
5. Close your eyes and imagine:

   - A black expanse.
   - An ornate double door like the kind you would find on a temple in Thailand.
   - Both doors slowly open to reveal a large, ancient, and ornate book sitting on an elegant golden pedestal.

Each page of this old book is a different parallel universe.

6. Lift the pages of the book with your left hand so you can let the pages flop down as you slid your thumb towards the first page in your hand, but don't start.
7. As you hold the pages, regain the feeling you made in step 2.
8. Monitor that feeling while letting the pages of the book slowly flop by. The universes of each page gives off its own feeling, but you don't need to feel each one.
9. When you come to a page that increases the feeling that you are holding, stop, leave the book open to that page.
10. Think, "This is the universe I am in now."
11. Leave the book open to that page and back out of the room.
12. Open you eyes.
13. Embrace anything in the real room that seems a bit different (the pattern of the wooden floor or table) as belonging to the universe where you would love to be, to come home to.

Welcome here.

The Body Electric

Consider the design of a robot where everything passes through a central feed: control signals, data, power, and of course damage reports. In addition to being an information conduit, this central feed is the main structural support for the robot. Now imagine that due to accidents and injuries there has developed along the central feed a number of bumps and bends. The bumps and bends put pressure on the control and feedback signals causing communication to degrade. This can lead to real trouble. Unfortunately, that's what a lot of us have. Our central feed is our spine. Our spine is essential to our health and physical condition. It is difficult to get in touch with your intuition when you are distressed by health problems, and it can be difficult to meditate when your spine is not in good alignment.

Learning how to ground the base of your spine is the beginning of gaining control over energy flow and learning block removal. Blocks are removed from the body through the spine. They are removed with a visualization that is actually considered a meditation and thus we come upon the interrelation between blocks and health. The proper shape of the spine is essential to meditation and block removal and is also the key to good health. In fact, in a fascinating though grisly study, performed by Dr. Henry Winsor, M.D., in cooperation with the Laboratory of Operative Surgery, at the University of Pennsylvania, autopsies were performed to search for minor pathological (structurally abnormal) curves of the spine and dysfunctional internal organs. An even 100 pathological curves were located. Examination of the internal organs of the bodies found that 96 of these pathological curves were directly related to dysfunctional organs. This relationship had to do with the nerves that serviced these organs. These nerves passed through the vertebrae damaged by the pathological curves. So even minor distortions in the shape of our spine need to be corrected.

In pictures of the great yogis meditating you can see the relationship between meditation and the spine. Their upper backs are straight, their shoulders are back, and still they appear relaxed. When you have meditated for a few months you will notice that you are automatically straightening your back as you try to find your "level" or "meditation spot". This is because most meditations are enhanced by, and at the same time promote, an energy flow through the spine. This energy flow is effected by the health and position of the spine and vice versa.

If you have a little trouble relating to the idea of body energy, consider acupuncture. The increased acceptance of acupuncture by the medical profession can be seen in the number of health insurance plans that now cover acupuncture treatments as an alternative approach to drugs and surgery. What makes this acceptance most significant is that acupuncture is based on restoring the natural energy flow of the body. The increased acceptance of this human energy flow is a real awareness breakthrough that is slowly spreading through all levels of society.

Sticking needles into the body is a rather shocking concept that gets attention and starts people talking. This attention is one of the reasons acupuncture has become well known. The real basis of acupuncture, energy flow, has no sensationalism to spur its recognition. Also, the energy flow concept is an easy target for the Contrarians since it is difficult to prove. The result is that the acceptance of the human energy flow concept will lag behind the acceptance of acupuncture. Its acceptance, however, is constantly increasing. More books are being written about it every year and it is being used successfully in many types of therapy.

The flow of energy through the spine is the most critical flow, since the spine is the central feed for the nervous system of our bodies. Problems with the spine can result in poor performance of our internal organs that take years to be recognized. This is one reason why problems with the spine need to be taken seriously. Another reason concerns blocks. Energy flowing through the spine is very effective in removing blocks. To get rid of blocks, your spine must be free to allow energy to flow through it in the most unrestricted manner possible. Physical problems with the spine retard the flow of energy and can make the removal of blocks difficult.

You may have already experienced a momentary problem with energy flow through your spine when you practiced your Grounding tool. If, at first, you couldn't seem to find a comfortable position or had a desire to straighten out your back, you were receiving a message that your spine was not in a position to allow energy to flow correctly. You were probably able to correct this by just moving around until you felt better. Maintaining a healthy shape to the spine is as essential to good health as it is to meditation and block removal. Unfortunately, we as Americans have, typically, poor posture. The excessive number of back problems in our country is testimony to this condition. In order to straighten out this problem we need to understand how it started.

Who Bent This Body?

Some highly industrialized countries, including the United States, have a much higher incidence of back problems than countries such as India, Greece and Portugal. Photographs of people in these different countries reveal that many people in countries with increased back problems hold their bodies in a way that causes a structurally unsound spine. This incorrect body position appears to be caused by a difference in the aesthetically desired body shape. This difference actually has to do with the differing levels of prosperity between countries.

To determine the correct body position for sitting, standing and bending over, you only need to look at young children. This is because young children have not yet developed a concern for appearance. It turns out that children tend to use a specific body position until a certain age. The age of change corresponds to the age when children begin to imitate the mannerisms of their parents. Comparing photographs of people in books like *Eternal India* by Indira Gandhi with *America and Lewis Hine* by Lewis Hine reveals that most people in India have the natural, child-like body position, while many people in the United States have adopted the unhealthy body position. So how did an unhealthy body position come to be considered attractive?

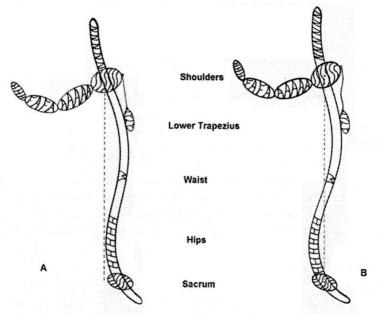

Figure 5. A -Upper torso is pulled out over the hips due to a taut stomach. B – Weight of upper torso is directly supported by the hips and sacrum.

Until the twentieth century it was considered desirable to be a bit heavy, a little plump. Being plump was a sign of the good life and posterity. However, during the modern era, in the more prosperous countries, plumpness fell out of style. People wanted to appear slender. They started holding in their stomach and tucking in their bottom.

Over time, this became more than just a fashion trend. As indicated by the photographic study, it created a permanent change in what was considered normal posture. The effect of that change has gone unnoticed by the mainstream medical industry, but it has not gone unnoticed by our bodies. Back pain is the way our bodies have notified us that we have taken a wrong turn.

Holding in your stomach can cause the following changes in the support structure of your body:

1. The natural curve of your lower back, which should be fairly deep, is flattened out. Refer to Figure 4. This functional drawing uses letters to indicate different areas, e.g., a chain of the letter "N" indicates the neck section of the spine and the letters "FA" indicate the forearm.
2. The loss of the lower curve and the tension of the stomach muscles causes an unnatural forward curve to your upper back.
3. The forward curve of your upper back moves your shoulders forward so they effectively hang over the center of your body.
4. This prevents the upper half of your body from resting directly over your hips and lower back. Therefore, part of the burden to support your upper body is transferred to your lower trapezius muscles (mid back).
5. Your lower trapezius muscles will be constantly pulled by the weight of your shoulders which are forward of the centerline of your body (hanging over). In order for your back to remain straight, the lower trapezius muscles must constantly pull against the weight of your shoulders.

When you are younger and your back muscles are stronger, they can constantly pull at the weight of your shoulders without too much trouble: The only time you will feel uncomfortable is when you try to sit in one place for a long time in a chair without a back or stand. However, when you get older your muscles weaken. What in your youth was only mid-back muscle tension can now turn into mid-back muscle spasms. If only one side spasms, your spine can be pulled severely out of shape and pathological curves of the spine may result. (Pathological curves of the spine are curves that are structurally abnormal.)

The unhealthy posture (little or no natural curve in the lower back) is a structurally weaker shape for your spine to maintain. Even if you never experience any back spasms you drastically increase the chances of back injury if your back structure is weak. This weakness can allow minor injuries to have permanent effects on the shape of your spine, distorting it even further, and causing more problems. This may be the major reason for the number of back problems that Americans experience. I am no exception.

I have been an active gymnast for many years, with the exception of my college years, when I went into competitive swimming and springboard diving. In addition to gymnastics I am an avid rock climber, body surfer, rollerblader.... If it's dangerous and strenuous, I like it, but I get injured often as a result. I emphasized gymnastics because if you ask ten retired gymnasts why they stopped, nine will tell you, "too many injuries" (it is a non-contact sport but the floor doesn't seem to play by the rules). I have been able to continue doing gymnastics much longer than most because I take responsibility for healing myself. When I have a problem, I study and research and treat myself until I have exhausted all avenues. I had a back problem for 20 years. That's how long I have been trying different theories for back problems.

With two exceptions, I have been very successful with self-healing. Those two exceptions turned out to be tremendous learning experiences. The less serious injury was from a 1979 hang gliding crash, where my right shoulder got banged up. Weeks after the crash it was still hurting. I went to a doctor who said that the only thing they could do was apply ultrasound. This was unsuccessful. I was unwilling to accept that there was nothing else that could be done. I decided to take responsibility for my own healing. I studied how the shoulder worked and the possible causes for my pain. I finally found a stretch that relieved the discomfort, but it took 8 years. During that time I learned the tremendous value of steady, gradual, relaxed stretching. This type of stretching has helped keep me young. If you are looking for a fountain of youth, try daily stretching. Never bounce or pump the area you stretch; just relax and visualize the tendons and muscles becoming longer and longer. If you want to accelerate the effects of your stretching, find out about isometric stretching.

In 1966 I injured my back by opening up too late on a front one and a half somersault on a trampoline. The resultant crash started off with my face impacting the trampoline at great speed and finished up with my feet trying to hit me in the back of the head. I felt like second runner-up in the new game show Pretzel For a Day. I developed a pinched nerve in my lower back. This was so painful that I quit gymnastics and joined my college's swimming team because everybody said that swimming was good for your back. Many long and wet miles later, I finally admitted that swimming couldn't stop my back from going out when I bent over incorrectly or laid down in the wrong position. This turned out to be very embarrassing one night in the back of my father's car. My date's father had to come and drive us home from the drive-in. You bet I learned everything I could about back injuries, and yet to no avail. After a while I discovered how to put my spine back in place by myself, but I was still plagued by it going out whenever I did something wrong.

One of the things I love to do was apparently very wrong. I love to windsurf in the San Francisco Bay or the ocean, in strong wind. Every time I would come in after crashing through the wind driven chop and seas my back would be out. I was usually successful in getting it back in, but I always suspected that it was not the crashing that put it out, but the bending over for twenty minutes when I was putting the equipment together.

After twenty years I finally discovered a solution. I learned a new way of standing, sitting, and most important, bending over. The next time I went windsurfing, I assembled my equipment by bending this new way. After I finished crashing around in the bay for two hours, I knew I was on to something good. My back felt fine. I was able to apply this new concept to almost all of the many movements that I use in my athletics. In a few months I became stronger and more comfortable inside my body. I applied this to sitting and found that my meditations were better and that blocks were much easier to remove.

Getting in Shape

The following instructions are general guidelines. They may not be right for your particular body type, especially if you have some extreme features, like a large belly. Some modifications may be required and in some cases these instructions will simply not be the right approach. However, most of you will profit greatly from considering these gentle changes in the way you operate your body.

The Standing Exercise

Do this whenever you are standing still, such as waiting in line:

1. Distribute your weight such that 70% is being supported by your heals.
2. Tilt your hips such that the top of your hips tilts forward and the lower portion moves back (stick out your buttocks). This puts the correct curve in your lower back and allows you to relax your stomach muscles without your stomach sticking out any more than it did before.
3. Rotate each shoulder (one at a time) forward, up, back and then down. Keep them in this back and down position for the rest of your life or whenever you want to feel good.

In the beginning it feels like you are standing really weird, but if you look in the mirror you will see that you do not look any stranger than before. Do not concern yourself about relaxing your stomach. I personally have been holding my stomach in for about thirty years. Talk about trouble letting go. It turned out that my reluctance to let it all hang out was unfounded. Clothes make a much larger impact on your apparent shape than stomach tension. Avoid pants with pleats and tight shirts (especially short-sleeves) and you will look just fine.

Posture and Energy

Many people come home from work too tired to enjoy their lives. Why do people get so tired from office work? What is strenuous about sitting, talking, typing, and a little walking? People must be doing these things wrong if it is making them tired, considering that our ancestors were able to work the fields from sun up to sun down. True, stress will contribute to fatigue, but the way you sit and hold yourself is also taking its toll.

One of the things we do at work that makes us tired is raise our shoulders. The next time you are hurrying down a hall at work, see if you can lower your shoulders. If you can, your neck muscles were in tension. This tension is a reaction to pressure: "I have to do this. I have to do that." The body language message that this posture is sending out is, "Don't bother me, I am very busy." This message may be exactly what we want to send out, but the cost of the message, tension, is too high. The tension that starts in your neck can spread down your entire back. Keeping such a large area tense can make you very tired by the end of the day.

Keeping your shoulders down and your neck muscles relaxed is an easy way to maintain your energy at work. People who type have an additional problem in this area. There is an unfortunate hold over from the days of the manual typewriter. Back then you were taught not to rest your forearms on the desk so you could hit each key with the same force. This is what makes typing so tiring. Check it out. With your left arm resting on your desk, place your right hand on the muscle that connects the side of your neck and your shoulder. Now raise your left hand off the desk as if it were poised over a keyboard. Feel the tension in that muscle? Holding both your arms like this produces constant muscle tension. There is no longer any need to hit keys with the same pressure. We have electronic keyboards. Rest your forearms on the desk. Better yet, put your keyboard on your lap and rest your forearms on the arms of your chair. If you can put your keyboard on your lap, you can sit back in your chair. You may need to glue a piece of fabric (felt works very well) to the bottom of the keyboard so it doesn't slip off your lap. If you use rubber cement, the fabric can be removed without messing up the keyboard. Putting the keyboard on your lap is the best ways to avoid CTS (carpal tunnel syndrome), also known as repetitive wrist injury, which is a very common disabling condition caused by pinching the medial nerve in the wrist. The reason this is such a wide spread problem is that most of the medical community doesn't understand the problem. If people could find a way to type without constantly holding their fingers up, CTS would be a problem of the past. Putting the keyboard on your lap allows you to let your hands dangle over the keys and relax them.

I developed this affliction ten years ago; it's a bummer. The operations, one on each wrist, which I initially thought were a success, were a fraud. The pinching of nerves is caused by swelling due to irritation from over-use. After the first operation I could not use my hand for weeks. However, the swelling takes months to escalate to be able to pinch nerves. After months of reuse the symptoms came back and the doctors said there was nothing else they could do. Different doctors, same old song. Again I had to figure out a solution and heal myself. Once I understood what the real problem was, I was able to develop therapies that relieved my symptoms. Among the most effective was to place my keyboard on my lap.

Years ago, when we had manual typewriters, CTS was almost unheard of. On these manual typewriters, you could rest your fingers on the keys without setting them off. With today's electronic keyboards and light touch, you must *constantly* hold your fingers up. The failure to recognize this difference is why carpal tunnel syndrome remains such a difficult problem. If you suspect that your wrist structure is susceptible, put the keyboard on your lap and rest your arms on the arms of your chair. If your arms are high enough, you will be able to relax your fingers over the keyboard. You may need to invest in a chair whose arm height and distance from your body can be adjusted, but such efforts are a better alternative to pinching nerves until you lose the use of your hand.

Now that you have learned to improve your stance, you may want to work on your walk, bending over, and sitting. The body position in all these is basically the same, but you may need to do things a little differently in order to maintain that natural curve in your spine.

The Walking Exercise

The idea is to keep your hips tilted and your stomach relaxed as in step #2 of the Standing exercise. With each step push yourself forward from the base of your spine and use the entire length of your leg to propel yourself forward. You may notice that you are able to walk faster with less effort than before.

Bending Over Bending

In bending over to work on something low, to wash your face or to pick up a heavy object, the important thing to remember is to tilt the top of your hips forward (stick out your buttocks). If you maintain a tilted hip position you will automatically maintain a curve in your lower back and a straight upper back.

The Sitting Exercise

A sure test of proper sitting posture: can you be comfortable sitting still for a long period in a chair that doesn't have a back, such as a stool or piano bench? This is something I could never do before I learned the correct curve for my spine. This was a real pain since I play piano. Once you have learned this exercise you will be able to sit longer and more comfortably and meditate better in any chair.

1. If the chair has a back, push your buttocks as far back into the seat as you can. Push it back. Push it back. Waaaaay back. If there is no back on your chair, pick yourself off the floor and start over. This time stop at the edge of the chair. Now tilt your hips as much as possible such that your stomach moves forward a bit.
2. With your shoulders back, lean forward to a 45 degree angle (chest half way to your knees) and put a curve in your lower back so that your weight shifts from your buttocks to your thighs.
3. Now sit back up, keeping your hips tilted and the curve in your lower back.
4. Relax your stomach and rotate your shoulders forward, up and back.

If you have had trouble performing some of the exercises, do not be discouraged. Just as when we are first learning a skill in sports, music, or crafts, some things seem impossible. After a while they become easier, and then, finally, simple.

When our body wants to send us a message that something is seriously wrong, such as a spinal problem, it can cause a block which may not be removable with visualizations. A few changes in your posture, chiropractic or physical therapy may be necessary.

6 – Block Busters

If you were in the perfect state of mind to access your intuition and someone were to ask you how you felt, you might answer that you felt nothing. Intuition, which usually manifests itself as a mild feeling, can be easily blocked by other feelings. To access your intuition accurately, these interfering feelings must be removed. This does not mean that you need to become an unfeeling, iron-willed cretin. In fact, it is important that you allow your emotions to run their course while you are addressing the related issue, and when you have experienced them for an appropriate amount of time, let them go. Completely. If you are unable to let a feeling go after a reasonable amount of time has passed (what constitutes "reasonable" will vary from issue to issue), consider seeking help outside of your own personal resources. There may be more going on there than you are aware of.

Intense emotional issues create interfering feelings that can last for a very long time. In most cases the noticeable part of these feelings eventually fades. However, if the issue is not resolved, feelings can remain below the level of your conscious awareness. This emotional residue, as well as more noticeable emotions, create blocks and need to be removed. You will soon learn a simple method of removing these and other blocks, long enough, if not permanently to use your intuition and make those important decisions.

The tools you will learn to remove blocks were developed from new age approaches to wellness. With them, you will be able to perform a similar clearing of energy channels that acupuncture accomplishes. As opposed to acupuncture you will not have to listen to the oldest lie of all: this wouldn't hurt. So, as you may have suspected, your intuition practice can have the additional benefit of improving your health in many ways.

Detecting Blocks

Some blocks are easy to detect; others are a bit elusive. For example, intense trauma like the grief of losing a loved one is experienced as real physical pain. You hurt in the center of your body. There is an ache that you can easily locate. Unfortunately, not all blocks are this easy to feel. Some simply feel like a slight weight. Some feel similar to an upset stomach. Some blocks feel like a slight headache. Many blocks cannot be felt at all without performing some awareness enhancing tool. This is why it is important to practice Present Time on a regular basis. Present Time will start to increase your sensitivity to the way you feel which is essential to locating blocks.

In addition to grief, mentioned above, other emotions that result in blocks include anxiety, anger, resentment, fear, guilt, and worry. Small amounts of each of these emotions can add up to a very effective block that will completely mask your intuition. Therefore, even if you have had few emotional incidents you should still check yourself closely for blocks before using your intuition.

Blocks caused by strong emotions can be easily detected. Weaker emotions cause blocks that are more difficult to find. In order to develop your ability to detect blocks, you should start with blocks caused by a strong emotion like a personal loss or disappointment. If it is not too disturbing, recall that loss while performing the Block Detection tool below. Do not be discouraged if you experience difficulty with this tool; you will be able to do it more easily with practice.

Block Detection Exercise

In order to use this tool, you need to be in a place where you will not be distracted.
1. Use a comfortable straight back chair. Sit up straight with both feet flat on the floor.
2. Close your eyes and get into Present Time and Center of Mind.
3. Think of an incident that will invoke a strong emotional reaction. This could be a loss, a failure, a frustration, or a strong resentment.
4. Find the exact location of this feeling.

5. Try to describe the feeling to yourself:
   How heavy or light does it feel?
   What color does it have?
   How large is it?
   Is there anything that distinguishes it from the rest of your body?

Once you become familiar with the different characteristics of blocks it will be easier to detect them. Practice detecting them when something occurs to you that could cause a block. Perform the Block Detection Exercise and try to find the block. Practicing how to find blocks is the best preparation for learning how to remove them.

Encourage yourself to use the tools in this book every day by treating them as recreation. Think of them as playing with the advanced powers of the subconscious mind. They can eventually make you feel very good and point out the direction to a more positive life. If you recognize them as activities that make you feel good, you will always be attracted to using them. So remember the good feeling you have when you finish using these tools.

Preventing Blocks

Even people who practice removing blocks daily cannot always keep themselves free of blocks. Sometimes you are just too closely surrounded by demands and emotions. Sometimes a block is being caused by a very disturbing issue that you are unable to immediately deal with. When I moved into my current house, I imagined that every box screamed "unpack me first". I would look at a box and think, I can't unpack this box because I want to put its contents on the shelves that I haven't put up yet, and I can't put up my shelves because I haven't unpacked my tools. I can't unpack my tools because I have no place to put them since I gave my old work benches away and I haven't built the new benches yet because. . . I wasn't getting unpacked, and I was certainly creating significant blocks with my anxiety.

What I needed more than anything during the unpacking was my small fan. At this point I had already developed a method of using intuition to find things. However, I couldn't get my intuition to work because of the large blocks that reappeared when I looked at my palace

148

of boxes. I spent 2 days looking for that fan, but to no avail. Then I called, a friend who has great natural intuition for finding things. When she came over, I told her that I thought it was someplace upstairs because most everything was. Less than 2 minutes later she came downstairs with my fan. The unpacked boxes didn't affect her because they weren't her problem so she could access her intuition.

If someone lived an idyllic life they would not create blocks. Unfortunately, our lives are more likely to contain a fair number of frustrations and problems. These frustrations are usually unavoidable and often cause blocks. However, there are some block causing scenarios that can be easily avoided. One of the most common is incorrect concern for a friend.

Sometimes when a friend or lover is hurt and you are unable to help, you respond by becoming miserable yourself then displaying your pain to your friend. Your friend does not want you to be in pain. If they see that they have done this to you, they are likely to feel even worse. So you have made yourself feel bad, your friend feel worse, and on top of that you are making a bunch of blocks for both of you.

Concern should inspire you to benevolent action, not cause you to suffer. Do something for your hurting friend that you know will warm their heart, such as read them a story or rub their back. Be happy you can help a friend. If you want to say something, say "I am sorry that you are hurting. Is there anything I can do to help you get through this?"

If you once used suffering to show your concern and now decide to adopt this new approach you may be criticized. Your friends who are sick or in pain may say, "You don't act like you care about me any more". When this happens it is time to explain that you realized they don't want you to feel bad when they are down, and that you want to care for them with your actions, by not making yourself feel bad. Explain that your feeling at peace will have a better effect on their well-being than if you suffered along with them.

Try to respond to things that cause bad feelings with little emotion, and to respond to positive things with great emotion. If you want to feel your intuition consistently, move away from negativity. Move into appreciation. Each day, remember something good that happened and when someone asks how your day was, tell them about that good thing.

Blocks that interfere with your intuition can be caused by unresolved emotional issues that you are not always aware of. The good news is that these blocks can be temporarily removed even though the issue still needs your attention. However, it is essential for your peace of mind that you eventually resolve the issues that created your blocks in the first place. Meditation can help you develop the self-awareness that will reveal these self-deceptions.

If you find yourself repeatedly getting into personal conflicts you may be addicted to the dramatic life that such behavior supplies. It may be hard to stop doing this; no addiction is easy to break. In this case you may not be able to access your intuition because of the blocks these emotions cause. You must deal with your addiction. Sometimes motivation to do this is only found during or after a prolonged period of bad health which this lifestyle tends to produce.

Another cause of blocks is the failure to meet responsibilities. If you avoid your responsibilities, the block will return time and again, regardless of how well you remove it. Even if you rationalize that the responsibility is not yours, your subconscious will see through the rationalization and the blocks will return.

In today's world, many of us have too many responsibilities to ever feel at peace. Some people have developed their self-awareness to the point where they are very conscious of how they feel. Some have given up high paying jobs, big houses, and fancy cars to reduce responsibilities so they can achieve peace of mind. This may appear a bit extreme to you now, but if you are overburdened with responsibilities, your health can be threatened and, of course, it will be difficult to keep blocks from forming. As you become sensitive to blocks you will notice more of them and you will most likely become aware of how previously unnoticed elements in your life adversely affect the way you feel. You may realize that it will be difficult to remove these elements from your current surroundings.

Removing Blocks

So far you have learned to be in Present Time, to get into Center of Mind, to recognize blocks, and to ground. The combination of these skills and the right state of mind are what is needed to remove blocks. The best state of mind to remove blocks (and to solve problems) is amusement. Consider buying a collection of your favorite comics: The Far Side or Calvin and Hobbes or whatever has the best chance of making you laugh out loud. Read from the collection until you laugh out loud and then use the deblocking tool below.

There is a great deal of information available concerning block removal, since it is a goal of many meditations. Some of this information suggests that block removal is difficult, even painful, and this is sometimes true if you use an inferior method. Being aware of your grounding will help you remove the blocks and insure that it is done safely.

Blocks caused by strong emotions should only be removed after these emotions have had their expression and have been allowed to move through you. Feeling pain and grief is an important part of the human experience, but if their effects linger (emotional residue), access to your intuition will be affected. When you learn how to remove blocks you will find that their removal can eliminate emotional residue and that "down" feeling that emotional residue often creates.

If you decide to learn some block removal tools and use them only when you want to use your intuition, you may have some trouble. Block removal tools are a little complicated and they are difficult to perform if you have not practiced. On the other hand, if you develop a habit of removing blocks on a regular basis and make a few changes in your lifestyle that will reduce your accumulation of blocks, you will find it much easier to remove them and keep them away. It is this elimination of blocks that will bring you the benefit of improved health. Removing blocks does not take long and you can do it anywhere.

The Deblocking Tool

Find a straight chair to sit in and assume the proper sitting position with your feet flat on the floor, hips tilted, shoulders back and stomach relaxed. Use the deblocking tool as follows:

1. Close your eyes and take a couple of deep breaths.
2. Relax by making every inch of your body as heavy as lead.
3. Ground and obtain Center of Mind.
4. Quiet your mind.
5. Locate blocks.
6. Take the top of the grounding cord and move it over to the location of a block and use it like a vacuum cleaner to suck the block down and out of your body through the grounding cord.

Since the grounding cord is attached to deepest earth, you can imagine that it has tremendous gravity and will pull the block down by this gravity alone. You may recognize a block as belonging to an old painful issue and feel pain somewhere in your body. Use the grounding cord to remove the pain just like removing a block. If you maintain a quiet mind during the use of this tool, you can consider this another meditation. This meditation can reduce pain from headaches and injuries. These types of meditations are so effective that people who are unable to take an anesthetic have used them to get through major surgery. Do not try this without professional help.

As with any visualization try to avoid forcing the images to remain in your mind's eye. It is best to simply allow them to unfold. Relax and allow yourself to be an observer, an observer from the center of your mind.

It may seem that you are having to use a lot of tools and haven't even thought about intuition, but there is relief in sight. Grounding will be combined with Center of Mind and removing blocks, so all three will be performed at once. Eventually you will only need to do these visualizations for a few minutes a day to keep your body clear and ready to reliably access your intuition. However, you may find the effect of the visualizations is so pleasant that you will want to increase this effect by doing visualizations for longer periods. If you have been reading quickly you may not have mastered a tool before another one is presented. If this is the case you may want to stop reading and practice the tools you have learned before you read the next section.

Meditation

Meditation is extremely effective in increasing one's sensitivity to intuition because it increases one's sensitivity to everything. Some people who meditate regularly find that drinking an once of wine makes them feel quite tipsy. There are many effective meditations. The only necessary requirement is that the meditation quiet the noisy mind that is in constant deliberation about the past or future, with what you should have said, what you should do, what is wrong with you, and so on. Find a meditation that appeals to you personally. Below are a few examples which are fairly easy to learn. As you meditate, keep in mind that it is not the normal state of your mind to cease its deliberations, therefore, it may revert to them often. Do not be dismayed. Simply allow your mind to follow its course for a moment and then gently return it to the meditation.

Different people need different amounts of meditation to achieve the same effect. Nevertheless, even a short amount of time spent meditating can be helpful. Of course the amount of benefit you receive will be in direct proportion to the amount of time you spend meditating. The average person wishing to improve their level of awareness and peace of mind should meditate for at least twenty minutes a day. A ten minute session may be sufficient to maintain your current level.

Twenty or thirty minutes may sound like a long time to sit and do nothing, but consider the amount of time you spend watching TV. Most people think nothing of watching a half hour of an upsetting news show that does little to improve their well-being and usually leaves them frustrated at some governmental incompetence or upset by the reported violence. Therefore, spending twenty minutes to increase your awareness and improve your mental and physical health is investing relatively little time considering the reward received. Try thinking of meditation as a reward or as something to do when you want to indulge yourself. Think of it as a substitute for a snack or something to make you feel good about yourself. If you love to take showers think of meditation as a mental shower, a shower in which you can stay for as long as you want.

The Yoga Meditation

This meditation is easy to teach but it can be challenging to maintain because there are no mental images upon which your mind's attention can be focused. Therefore, your mind can easily wander.

1. Sit as in the Sitting exercise.
2. Close your eyes, take a few deep breaths, and relax.
3. Focus your attention on a spot in the center of your forehead.
4. Keep your mind perfectly clear. Do not let any thoughts take hold. Concentrate only on the center of your forehead.
5. Do this for at least twenty minutes.

The group Ananda, headquartered in Nevada City, California, teach this type of meditation. Ananda's teachings aim to bring a person closed to God through meditation and other Yoga practices. Their practices do not conflict with Western beliefs since their use of the word God refers to a universal God. Ananda avoids defining or identifying God beyond ones own personal experience. However, members of Ananda have a strong reverence for the great Yogis whose philosophies they study. Ananda portrays these Yogis in a light similar to Western saints.

The Zen Meditation

In this meditation you concentrate on your breathing. This provides an effort to focus on and helps prevent your mind from wandering. Sit as in the Sitting exercise.

1. Close your eyes and relax.
2. Breathe from your stomach with emphasis on the exhalation. Exhale slowly until you feel like a bag that has completely collapsed. Your inhalation should feel relaxed. Simply allow your lungs to fill to their normal capacity.
3. Keep your mind perfectly clear. Do not let any thoughts take hold. Just breathe. If you are having difficulty, you can count your breaths up to ten and start over again.

4. Do this for at least twenty minutes.

Zen philosophies are among the most difficult to encapsulate without distorting them. The general aim of practicing Zen is liberation. As one of their great philosophers, Lao-tzu said, "Become unaffected; cherish sincerity; belittle the personal; reduce desires." The subject of God is not addressed. There is no central headquarters in the States for the practice of Zen; however most heavily populated areas have Zen meditation centers that are listed in the yellow pages under Churches, Buddhist.

The Chanting Meditation

This meditation uses repetitive sound to assist in quieting the mind. It is mentally easy but requires some conditioning of the throat. This conditioning occurs after a few days of chanting, but some people, singers for example, already have a conditioned voice. The chant is complex enough to occupy your mind, but not so complex that the higher levels of consciousness are engaged.

A twelfth century Japanese monk developed this chant, but it's practice was suppressed, even in Japan until the end of World War II. It is only in the past fifty years that it has become known outside of Japan. Since then it has gained world wide popularity. Proponents of the chant claim that it brings good fortune and an elevated zest for life. There is a world wide peace organization which places great power in the words of the chant and believes that by chanting you will discover how to obtain your goals and your own happiness. They believe that if enough people chant there will be no more war because there cannot be war if people are happy.

The chant consists of repeatedly saying the following:
Nom-myo-ho-ren-gay-kyo
The pronunciation is as follows:
Nom As in "Mom" but with an "n".
Myo The "m" sound, followed by "yo", as in yoyo. One long syllable.
Ho Same as "hoe" used in gardening.
Ren Same as the "ren" in the renaissance.
Gay Same as "gay" meaning happy.
Kyo The "k" as in key, followed by "yo", as in yoyo. One short syllable.

155

Directly translated:

Devotion to the cosmic law of cause and effect through sound

What you are saying when you chant is that you are willing to live in acceptance of the concept of what comes around goes around. In other words, your good actions or thoughts will eventually cause good things to happen to you. The same is true for bad actions or thoughts. By making the sound that represents this concept, you are affirming it. If you do not agree with this concept you should choose a different meditation.

This meditation encourages you to chant for the success of your goals and positive resolution of your problems by occasionally thinking of the outcome you would love to experience as you chant. You can contemplate a problem while you are chanting, and if a course of action comes to mind, it should be considered enlightened and likely to succeed. Although it is acceptable to think of these things, the most meditative effect occurs when you are simply listening to the sound of the words. If you want an eye opening experience, spend part of your chanting time matching the feeling of obtaining your desired outcome as you picture it.

Here is how you proceed with the chant meditation:

1. Sit as in the Sitting exercise.
2. Close your eyes, take a few deep breaths, and relax.
3. Chant in a monotone, supporting the syllables with your breath.
4. Listen carefully to your pronunciation. Quiet your mind and concentrate on the sounds you are making.
5. If desired, occasionally contemplate desires or problems and make the images that would occur when you have realized your desires or solved your problem. Create a feeling of success by using these images.
6. Continue chanting for ten to twenty minutes or whatever works for you.

At first you may find it physically difficult to chant for more than a couple of minutes. If this is the case, add a minute to your chanting each day or two. Your voice will develop the required strength and you will notice, should the occasion arise, that your singing improves. You may also find that chanting is very effective in removing anxiety.

There is something you should be aware of if you are going to try this chant. Chanting while imagining a certain outcome seems to increase the likelihood of that outcome, whether you believe it will or not. Therefore, it is extremely important that you do not worry (negatively visualize) about anything when you are chanting. Sometimes, when a person starts to practice this chant they have one calamity after another. This is a sure sign that you are having negative thoughts when you chant. Don't fall into this trap. Avoid all negative thoughts when you chant. If you notice any, immediately think of the corresponding positive outcome for twice as long and with strong feeling. Also, do not forget what you are affirming when you chant. Your good actions or thoughts will eventually cause good things to happen to you. The same is true for bad actions or thoughts.

If you want more information about this chant, the name of the organization that promotes it in the United States is known as SGI-USA. Its headquarters are in Santa Monica, California. Their philosophy contains no God type figures, therefore, it has little conflict with any religion. This philosophy promotes the belief that chanting, hard work, and the right attitude can turn any calamity into advantage.

Time To Meditate

Consider once again the amount of time you need to invest to improve your physical and emotional health. Is twenty minutes too much time to spend performing meditation and block removal if you can eliminate anxiety, gain full use of your mental capacity (at least the normal 20%), and empower yourself through access to your intuition? Of course not. Unfortunately, developing the meditation habit is not easy. You must truly love the benefits you perceive and have patience. What makes things even more challenging is that the morning is the best time to meditate. That means you must get up earlier. Arghhhhhhhhhhhh!

It is not easy to get up early because most people feel bad when they first get up. Putting off feeling bad is understandable, but you have to get up sooner or later. If you do it sooner you can meditate and be empowered for the rest of the day. Getting up early wouldn't feel so bad if you felt better when you get up. Any arguments? The key to feeling better when you get up is not how long you slept, but how gradually you come out of sleep. This is demonstrated by the fact that you feel the worst when you get up after being suddenly awoken from a deep sleep.

If you lie in bed most of the morning, you will eventually effect a gradual awakening. However, this is a very inefficient method of painless wakening and not at all necessary. Considering that you are unconscious and completely unaware, there can't be anything enjoyable about sleeping for a long period of time. Furthermore, over-sleeping can make you feel more tired (stagnant). Many times friends have complained to me about feeling tired and it turned out that they were sleeping more than usual. After a long trip people complain of "feeling tired", but in actuality they have been sitting still (resting) for hours. They are actually over rested. The most energetic people I know, sleep less than eight hours a day. You may think you need that much, but most people can adjust to less and feel better once they adjust.

There is one pleasurable part of sleeping, dreaming. Although everyone loves a good dream, they only last a few minutes, and sleeping longer does not have much effect on how long you dream. Nobody really enjoys all those unconscious hours; they simply hate getting up because they feel so stagnant. How much you sleep only has a slight effect on how you feel when you wake up. If you only sleep a little during the night you may not feel the results until later that day or the day after. How suddenly you wake up has a much stronger effect on how you will feel. Here are a few ideas that may help you get up earlier and feel better:

1. Put a small light on a timer and set it to come on fifteen minutes before you get up. Better yet, sleep with your blinds or drapes open, provided that it gets light a little before you want to get up. With either method your body will start coming out of deep sleep before you have to fully waken.
2. Get up at the same time every day. We all have natural clocks. If we get up at the same time each morning our bodies will start the waking process a little early, and we will therefore not be shocked out of a deep sleep.
3. If you go to bed late one night and want to make it up, go to bed early the next night, do not sleep later. Always wake up at the same

time, especially on the weekends. Do you want to spend you free time unconscious? Aren't you unconscious enough at work?

4. Upon waking perform mild exercise such as stretching, walking around, or just taking a shower. Realize that you are not feeling tired, you just spent hours resting, you are feeling stagnant. To get your body to stop feeling bad, you need to increase your circulation and flexibility. After hours of not moving the last thing you need is to sit in one place and tune in to how badly you feel. If you decide to do some exercises, start out with light ones with very few repetitions. Have some fruit, apples wake you up more than caffeine.

5. Take a short nap at the middle of your waking day. Many people feel tired at this time, but it is not usually physical fatigue. Your mind simply wants to break its bonds of regimented thinking with a dream or two. It only needs the freedom of a few minutes to feel revitalized. Do not take a long nap. A well fed human who has been doing light to moderate work only needs ten minutes rest to get back 90% of their energy. A long rest will make you feel stagnant. You don't want to feel terrible twice a day, do you? If you do feel stagnant after your nap, try eating something warm or having some caffeine.

6. You will feel better when you wake up if you do not go to bed with a full stomach. This is also bad for your digestion and will tend to make you gain weight.

7. Try eating or drinking something as soon as you get up. The best thing is a glass of water or a piece of fruit. For some people this is impossible. For others it can make them feel better very quickly. It works best if you did have an empty stomach when you went to bed.

8. For additional motivation, consider the person who only sleeps six hours a night. After forty years, they will have experienced five more years of conscious life than the person who sleeps eight hours a night. *Five years.*

Caffeine is a mild stimulant that can get you going, but taking it hot can be more relaxing than stimulating. If you want to wake up quickly or stay awake, have your caffeine cold. If you want to reduce your caffeine, have a warm, non-caffeine drink in the morning. In the morning you have many methods to get yourself going and the time to execute them.

Caffeine can be of more use for the afternoon slump when you are too busy to do other wake up activities.

Now that you are awake you may need some motivation to actually meditate. Companies spend thousands of dollars for large billboards along the freeways in order to influence you. Signs work. Consider writing down your goal and commitment in your own words or use something like, "I want to feel good. Meditation feels good. I want to meditate today and everyday." Tape it inside your medicine cabinet or some other place where you will see it when you first get up. If you are not ready for a full power meditation right away or if you missed your morning meditation you can use Present Time while you perform a simple task. The most rewarding task to combine with Present Time is eating.

Regardless of the meditation you choose, you will place yourself in the best frame of mind to meditate if, just before you start, you recall a pleasant occurrence from the previous day. It should not be something important, since you will most likely reflect on those things often enough. It should be something simple, like the smell of the air when you went out during lunch for example. This practice will also start you looking for things to appreciate during the day and you will strive to remember them, thus increasing your appreciation of life.

Before long, meditation will become its own motivation. The longer you have the meditation habit, the more easy it is to remember to meditate. Sometimes, you may forget or become too busy to meditate. When this happens, you may notice that you don't feel as good as you did before. Another type of motivation is to realize that daily practice seems to reduce the effort it takes to sit down and meditate; so don't miss a day.

Running Energy

The Running Energy meditation is similar to the Deblocking tool, with some additional visualizations.

1. Complete steps 1 through 6 of the Deblocking tool and return the top of the grounding cord to the base of your spine.

2. Remain in the center of your mind and imagine the space high above your head, out among the stars. This space is full of cosmic energy. Allow this energy to flow down to you and enter through the top of your head and travel down the back of your body to the base of your spine, and all the way down your grounding cord.
3. Imagine that the earth is full of energy, and let this energy flow up your legs, mix it with cosmic energy at the base of your spine, and let it flow down your grounding cord.
4. Now imagine that the combined energy of the earth and the cosmos flows up the front of your body and out the top of your head.
5. Imagine that this combined energy divides at your shoulders and that some of it runs down your arms and flows out the up-turned palms of your hands.

If you have trouble maintaining these images, you can have a friend make a visualization tape. Each of the instructions can be read onto the tape with five second pauses in-between. After this, repeat abbreviated instructions every 15 or twenty seconds such as; see the cosmic energy, see earth energy and cosmic energy mix and flow down your grounding cord, from the center of your mind see the grounding cord. To enhance the effect of the tape use a background sound of a gently flowing stream. Just make sure you visit the bathroom before listening to such sounds.

Running energy, grounding, and center of mind are similar to techniques taught by the Berkeley Psychic Institute in California. Students of the institute practice these techniques in preparation for using their psychic abilities. The institute offers classes on meditation, healing, and clairvoyance around the San Francisco Bay area. Their publisher, Deja Vu, also of Berkeley, carries their books on these subjects.

7 – Accessing Your Intuition

People like us, who believe in physics, know that the distinction between past, present, and future is only a stubbornly persistent illusion.

Albert Einstein

This chapter contains new terms to help you learn the final intuition technique quickly. In the same day that you learn the technique you will see the proof for yourself provided you have practiced the initial tools.

Transition Points

The transition point is the key to using your intuition. You will soon learn how to detect the point where success turns to failure by becoming aware of a change in the way you feel, but of course we need a name for that point.

The structure of a fine acoustic guitar is a precarious balance between strength and lightness. If a guitar is not made strong enough to withstand the tension of the strings (about half a ton), the top will warp. If the guitar is made too strong, the top will not vibrate enough and the guitar will sound dead. The shape of the support ribs that are glued to the underside of the top control the strength of the top.

The most critical moment in the construction of a guitar occurs when the craftsman is shaping the ribs. Their length and thickness is predetermined, but he must remove considerable wood from the top edge of each end, making the finished rib look like a bridge.

For the finest instruments, no measurements are taken for this most critical shaping. The craftsman removes wood with quick strokes of a carving tool until he thinks he should stop. If he stops too soon, the guitar will sound noticeably inferior. As he continues to remove wood, he reaches a point where the future of the guitar is changed. If he stops removing wood at this point the future of the guitar will be good. If he continues removing wood past this point the guitar top will be too weak and eventually warp. This point, where the success of a venture is determined, is the transition point.

The Connection

Consider the phenomenon of positive visualization. When you visualize a successful outcome, you increase its likelihood. The significance of this is that the visualization affects the outcome of a future event. Therefore, a connection exists between what we create with our mind and the future event. At first glance this connection appears to operate in only one direction, but appearances are not always accurate. It may be possible to take advantage of this connection in a backward direction.

Have you even done something that appears right, but you suddenly feel that there has been a change for the worse? It might happen when you are looking for a street to a person's house to which you have never gone. You are feeling excited about visiting them and not paying close attention to the directions. Because of this lack of attention you don't realize that you just passed the street. A moment later you feel something has changed. Later, when you find the street, it turns out that you had passed it just when you felt something change. This is the connection working in a feedback mode, but working backwards.

The same connection that allows you to affect the success of a future event with your mind's image may have allowed you to feel the future success of finding your friend's house. The success became invalid when you went past the correct street. The connection may have allowed you to sense the change in the success of the search effort. This possibility deserves contemplation, investigation, and experimentation because of the potential value of such feedback. Consider the following examples of this concept and try to project other useful applications.

Feelings of Validity

The following paragraph is the most important in this book. If you don't understand it at first, reread.

If, during the guitar's strut shaping, the craftsman were to imagine that the guitar was finished and visualize a beautiful sounding instrument that lasts many years, he would have a pleasant and powerful feeling, but what might happen to that feeling when he goes past the transition point as he is shaping the rib? Surely the validity of that feeling would change. Is it possible that he would notice this change in validity which occurs at the transition point?

Imagine it's Saturday night. Your favorite friends are over and you are cooking. In your mind you visualize a great dinner. Roast beef cooked to perfection, stir-fried vegetables fully cooked and not soggy, and garlic bread toasted in the oven until golden brown. There is a point in time for the cooking of the roast beef, the transition point, past which your friends will be lying to you, "It's not overdone". Under their breath they'll be saying, "We'll just give the end pieces to your pit bull. He can chew through anything". The vegetables have a transition point that you can see as you stir them around, no problem. Toasting the garlic bread has a transition point which we all know is approximately 2.3 microseconds long. No kitchen timer is that accurate. From all the burnt garlic bread we have hidden in the trash we know that only a wizard could open the oven door at the transition point of garlic bread. Or could you?

I prefer those dough-in-a-can, bake'em yourself biscuits. You break open the can/package, pull them apart, and throw them into the oven. I don't like to have to look on the package for the baking directions; I'm afraid I might notice the ingredients of those things. I can remember they bake at 350 like practically everything else and I don't need to know how long they say to bake them. I don't use timers, but I do match the feeling of a well cooked biscuit and fill myself with a golden light. I keep aware of that feeling as I cook a meal. As a guy whose favorite form of entertainment is having friends over and cooking for them and discussing the intricacies of life, you would think that my friends often witness burnt offerings. Such is not the case. I rarely burn anything.

At this point it is imperative that you consider the possibility of being able to feel the change in the validity of an imagined feeling. Consider the possibility of feedback. Try to remember some incident when, for no apparent reason, you had a feeling that the outcome of your venture had just gone sour. For example, you were imagining that the party that you are driving to will be great, but then you pass a street and that feeling changes. Up ahead, is that the Twilight Zone or did you just pass your turn?

Matched Feelings

If you remember the last time your date was an hour late, or your boss insisted that you do something really dumb. you can easily become angry. If you remember a beautiful sunset, you can easily feel calm. If you imagine a very successful outcome for a current project, you can feel like celebrating. A matched feeling is the latter, imagining the successful outcome and allowing yourself to feel the elation that such a success will instill.

Crinks and Sums

In order to recognize the change in validity of a feeling, you must become familiar with the usual state of the feeling. This is why you have been asked to solve problems by matching the feeling of success. The feeling of success, which you matched during problem solving, and the feeling of validity are basically the same feeling. This is why it is necessary to use the problem solving procedure in this book before you attempt to learn the intuition technique. The detection of the change in the validity of a matched feeling is the crucial operation in using the intuition technique. The most important step in learning this operation is understanding what to expect when the feeling of validity changes. Unfortunately, there seems to be no single word in the English language that describes exactly what you will feel when a matched feeling becomes invalid. It is like a feeling that something has shifted its location inside of you, or there is a drop in power or intensity of the feeling, or the euphoria in the matched feeling decreases. The detection of the transition point is not as hard as one might think, increasing your sensitivity by meditating, removing blocks, and running energy will make it much easier.

One word that comes close to the feeling of a matched feeling becoming invalid is "wrinkle"-a wrinkle that affects the whole feeling. A less used word that also comes close is "chink." Chink means a small fissure or crack, as in "chink in the armor." Both of these words combine to form a new word whose sound instills just the right feel: "crink." The word crink would be used as follows: a crink occurred in the matched feeling.

When you start using your intuition regularly you will notice that the most common occurrence of a crink is at a transition point *when* the proper action is not taken. This is a very useful tool if you know what the next step is but do not know when to take it. To ensure your success, be ready to execute the next step as soon as you go past the crink. Executing the step exactly after the crink, is usually successful even if timing is fairly critical.

A crink can also occur under slightly different circumstances. Let us say that you are making a decision that will affect the outcome of the event you are matching; if you go through the motion of making the wrong decision, you can detect the same type of crink. The converse is also true; if you go through the motion of making the right decision, you can detect an increase in the good feeling of what you are matching. This increased good feeling is called a "sum" and would be used as follows: a sum occurred in the matched feeling.

Sometimes it is better to try to detect a sum when you are making a decision because of its positive nature. However, a crink is usually easier to detect than a sum, perhaps because we allow the trauma of failure to be stronger than the rewards of success.

The Stop

The best way to practice detecting a crink is to use an operation that needs to be stopped at a specific time (the transition point) in order to ensure a good outcome. It is important that the act of stopping the operation is not complicated so you can concentrate on detecting the crink, not preparing to perform the stop. The task should not be so important that missing the transition point will cause a disaster. You don't want worry (negative visualization) to arise and cloud your intuition.

The day you pick to start your training is very important. You should pick a day when you will not be working or going to school. Do not plan to do a lot of things during the day. These plans often create pressure that can interfere with intuition. By now you realize how important it is that you start off this day with a good meditation and block removing session.

Day One

Let's go through a typical day and find operations you can use for practice. You may think that some of these operations are too insignificant to go through the bother of matching a successful feeling. In a way you're right, but if you select insignificant things, you will not have any fear of failure to overcome. Also, you must keep your intuitive decision-making skill sharp if you are to use it for important decisions so get into the habit of using it for the small things. Relying on your intuition whenever you can and inventing additional ways to take advantage of it will allow you to do it faster and with less effort.

You will start your training by applying intuition procedures to low risk decisions. Cooking is a very good for intuition practice and an excellent way to lose weight. Who likes burnt food? Actually, I have been cooking by intuition for years and none of my friends have died from it. Yet, cooking is probably the most common use of intuition, but most intuitive cooks are not aware of their ability. As you get better at using intuition you will start to gain back the weight you lost and your confidence will grow with your waistline.

From this point forward you will learn more and more advanced intuitive tools like finding lost articles. Eventually you will gain enough confidence to use intuition to make important decisions.

Cereal Milk – Before you start to pour your milk onto the cereal, match the feeling of being very proud of finishing the bowl and having exactly the right amount of milk. Fill yourself with the golden light of that success. As you pour, do not pay attention to the level of milk in the bowl. Begin pouring the milk and monitor the matched feeling, feel the light. Stop pouring when you think you feel a crink.

Shaving Cream – Before you push the button of the shaving cream, match the feeling of perfectly covering the area to be shaved with the exact right amount of shaving cream. Now push the button while maintaining that feeling. Stop pushing when you feel a crink.

By now you should have grasped the idea of using intuition for dispensing quantities. The following are operations similar to the two above in that they do not normally require the use of measuring cups or spoons: practice with these types of measuring operations first. Keep your mind open for these types of operations as you go through your day. Be creative.

- Paint Thinner – Match a beautiful finish and easy application.
- Plant Water – Match a large, healthy plant.
- Detergent – Match clean sparkling clothes and just pour. Relax, and wait for the crink.

As you get confident with using your intuition for measuring non-critical things (things that you don't have to measure with cups or spoons), you can start to use intuition for critical things. The following are things that are typically measured closely:

- Spices – Match a perfectly seasoned dish.
- Pancake Milk – Just like cereal milk.
- Nails – Don't count them just grab an amount that feels right. Don't grab too hard. Match finishing the job with no nails left over.
- Rice – Match everyone getting just enough rice.
- Rice Water – Match the rice coming out just right with no water left. This is an advanced skill since there are probably a few ruined dinners in your past due to badly cooked rice. Relax. Don't let visualizing those old failures interfere with your crink detection.

By now you might have some idea how my friend measured the string to fix exactly around the expectant mother's stomach. She matched the feeling of winning with her string being exactly the correct length, filled herself with a golden light and pulled the string through her fingers. When she felt the crink she stopped pulling and cut the string right there. If she could cut the string to match exactly, you can pour the rice water exactly.

So now that you have knocked around the house all morning pouring everything into all the containers you have, it's time for lunch. Looks like you will have to eat out of the box.

Setting Dials and Things

Perhaps you decide to fry something that you have never cooked before, and for which   the burner setting will be critical. Match a perfectly fried dish and start turning the burner knob. Stop when you feel the crink. Be creative. Find other setting operations.

Cruising

It's time to head out on the open road. However, when you get to the freeway you find the open road is not so open – there is some traffic. Try to use your cruise control anyway. Match the feeling of being very pleased at not having to adjust your speed for a long time because you had picked the exact right speed. Now speed up or slow down (whichever is called for) and monitor your matched feeling. Press the cruise control at the crink.

VCR

When you get home check the TV schedule and see if there is anything you might be able to stand watching. Do not watch it. Instead, record it on your VCR. When the show is recorded, rewind the tape and start watching it. When a commercial comes on, assuming that you are free of blocks, proceed as follows:

1. Close your eyes so you don't see the commercials running by at high speed – that's cheating.
2. Push the fast forward button.
3. When the tape is forward winding, match the feeling of stopping the tape at the exactly end of the commercials. Turn this feeling into the golden light of success. Fill yourself with this light. Feel the light.
4. Push the play button at the crink.

Big Decisions

You should practice using crink detection on less significant decisions before moving on to more important ones. The skill you develop with the less significant decisions will give you confidence you need to remain calm during an important decision. Once you have developed your skills, you can keep your intuition reliable by using it often. Use it every day.

If you are having difficulty with the tools or when you are about to measure something important, you should do Center of Mind and Present Time. If you feel good, proceed, but if you feel some disquieting sensations, you might have a block or two. You need to get rid of them since they represent an interfering feeling.

Once you have been practicing intuitive decision-making for a couple of weeks, you will have realized the value of having a body free of disquieting feelings. At this time your reliability using intuition should have increased to the point where you have complete confidence in your ability. These decisions can have some additional verification such as experiencing the transition point a number of times from different directions. The tool that will allow you to do this is called Finger Point.

Finger Point

Many decisions have only two choices: do it or don't do it, the cheap one or the expensive one, fix the old one or buy a new one, sell now or hold on to it.... The most reliable method of making this type of decision is to try to detect both a crink and a sum. This way, one feeling validates the other. This is not as hard as it seems since you make the decision slowly and detect the crink and sum at different times. The tool used to detect both feelings during a decision is called Finger Point.

Finger Point is a tool that will allow you to slow down the intuitive decision-making process and increase the accuracy of crink and sum detections. It will also allow you to repeatedly detect a crink or sum during a number of attempts. Here is an example:

You found the year and make of the used car you were looking for. It has a couple of problems that would not be too bad if there are no "surprises" after you have owned it for a while. You know there is usually a surprise or two. You are torn between buying the car and walking away. Deciding to use intuition, you drive to a quiet street, park your old clunker, and take out a piece of paper. On the left side of the paper you write "buy it". On the right side you write "run." Then you close your eyes, relax, and remove blocks. Next, you match the feeling of having owned your next car (whatever it turns out to be) for many years and it has proven to be a great investment. With your eyes still closed, hold your hand over the paper, point your finger to the right, and slowly move it to the left. Move it back and forth. Where is your finger when you feel the crink? Where is your finger when you feel the sum?

It is not necessary to write down the alternatives; you can just remember which side stands for what and move your finger back and forth in mid air. However, if you use the paper you can consciously forget which side is which and concentrate on detecting a crink or sum.

With this tool you can effectively make the decision many times without any risk. However, the most powerful crinks and sums occur with the first few motions from side to side. Therefore, to be most accurate, decide to only make a few passes.

Use Finger Point when you are in a book store looking for a good book. If you are looking for a certain type of book you can go to that section in the store and run your finger along the books trying to detect a crink. At the same time, you should match the feeling of going home, reading the book for a while, and realizing that it is a wonderful book. If you don't know what type of book you would like to read, you can find the section of the store the same way you look for a lost object. *Happy hunting.*

Use Finger Point when you have a group of things from which you must pick only one. Write your choices in a single column leaving a line or two between each choice. You can tape multiple pieces of paper together to give you more room. To make your selection:

1. Close your eyes.
2. Fill yourself with a golden light.
3. Imagine the desired outcome.
4. Feel the joy that the desired outcome will produce.
5. Run your finger down the list feeling for the crink or sum.

Finger Point Practice

The Finger Point provides the best opportunity to practice. This practice can provide you with feedback concerning your progress towards piece of mind. To practice:

1. Close your eyes.
2. Fill yourself with a golden light.
3. Imagine the desired outcome.
4. Feel the joy that the desired outcome will produce.
5. Run your finger up and down a blank piece of paper. You should feel a steady feeling of the joyful outcome.

If you do not feel a steady feeling, try:

♦ A few deep breaths
♦ Relaxation exercises
♦ Getting better control over worry and fear

Lost and Found

To find anything simply match the feeling of finding whatever you lost and fill yourself with golden light. Point your finger in different directions, thinking to yourself that you will look in that direction. Follow the sum. Stop at the crink.

Gambling Especially Roulette

A ball falling into a slot on a wheel is a real event so you can get a feel for where the ball will land. Stand at a roulette table and look at the red/black betting area. Red is usually on the left, black is on the right. How convent for using finger point.

Gambling on the Internet is much more difficult. The condition of a few bits in some unseen computer is not as significant as the falling of a physical ball. If you want to bet online, consider betting on horses or dogs. They are more real.

If you want to use finger point for roulette remember that the longer you play, the more fear is likely to interfere. I usually only place five to ten bets of around ten dollars, but I play the first, second, and third 12 (just above the red and black). These locations on the roulette table are very wide and allow my finger a lot of travel time so I can get a good feel for each position. Also, you win twice as much on the 12s.

Casino managers have the right to decide who plays. They will ask you to leave if you consistently win big. So don't go to the same casino two times in a row. Always leave a table if people start betting with you, their fear will interfere with you. Don't sit down, if you sit, you are obligated to place a bet, you don't need any extra pressure. Don't let your friends know what you are doing unless you know they believe you can do such things.

I have a friend who knows what I can do. She likes to hide a piece of candy in one of her hands and hold both hands in front of her. Then, I have to guess where the candy is. I can feel which hand has the candy and very rarely miss, but one night I couldn't tell any difference between her hands. I pushed them further apart and scrunched up my face in consternation. Finally, I just made a guess and slapped one hand in frustration. It was clear to her that I could not tell which hand the candy was in. She opened both hands to reveal candy in each. So when you having trouble with finger point on the roulette table, put a little money on 0 and 00. They are not red, black, or within the three 12 sets.

Some of my friends know that I always win at roulette and don't understand why I don't just gamble for a living. I have many reasons among them: it is not productive or creative, there is no interaction with others, it would not keep me sharp like my current work, and when the mortgage payment depends on the bets I place, it becomes more and more difficult to prevent fear from interfering.

Stock Selecting

This is really the best form of gambling and a great way to use finger point on a list. Your list of stocks should come from a trusted source. For example, I have been watching Martin Weiss who writes the Safe money reports. From 1999 to 2003 he has been very accurate. Also, his company rates all major stocks, bonds, companies, and even banks. Therefore, you can develop a huge list of winners of losers (if you want to purchase futures).

No matter which stock advisor you choose, all you need is a list of stocks you have some confidence in. Use finger point to pick the best stock. After you have made your purchase you can make a list of dates to allow you to use finger point to determine the best time to sell. Of course you should not use finger point to invest your hard earned money until you have developed skill and confidence by working with less important decisions.

New Life

Have you thought of some more possibilities for these tools? Yes, the possibilities are limitless. Although the major part of your training is finished, there are a couple of tools you should learn for the more important decisions and a few philosophical points I would like you to consider.

Now that you have learned how to get into Present Time and Center of Mind you do not need to practice them, only use them. At least every morning and every evening, take a moment to breathe deeply, relax, get into Present Time and Center of Mind, and check how you feel. If there is something that feels like a block, ground yourself and remove it. The more often you do this, the easier it becomes and the more sensitive you will be to the way you feel. It only takes four or five seconds to check yourself in this manner, and perhaps a couple of minutes to remove a difficult block if you feel one. This is not much time and is the absolute minimum practice you can do in order to keep your skills sharp.

I hope you did try a meditation and that you have been successful with the meditation of your choice. Success in meditation is easy to gauge. If you continue to meditate each day, you are a success. Success in obtaining Center of Mind and grounding are a little harder to judge. One verification of your success is an involuntary deepening of breath at the beginning of the visualization. If you find that you start breathing more deeply without consciously initiating it, then it is most likely that you have reached the correct state of mind. If you do not change your breathing involuntarily, it is not a sign of failure; your breathing may just be more efficient than others.

Helping Others

At this point you may be good at staying grounded and performing other functions like Running Energy. If you have developed your grounding well, you can use it in a very benevolent way. Grounding not only allows you to talk, think, and listen more clearly, but it can help others accomplish the same. Simply ground yourself and then visualize a grounding cord from the base of the other person's spine down into the earth. It can help to unobtrusively direct the palms of your hands towards the person.

You can ground people who have lost their train of thought or who can't remember something they wanted to say. You will find that it is surprisingly effective. Opening your mouth a little and breathing more deeply will increase your ability to hold the image of their grounding cord. If you hold your palms towards the person in mock stretching, it is easy to breathe deeply with your mouth open and appear natural. It is a wonderful feeling to help people out at embarrassing moments. It feels powerful and benevolent at the same time. A rare and most pleasant combination.

Knowing What You Eat

One result of becoming more sensitive to the way you feel is an increased awareness of the effect different foods and drinks have on your body. This will enable and motivate you to avoid things that are not good for you. After meditating for awhile you may realize that caffeine hurts you more than you had previously thought. Because of this knowledge you may be able to stop using it without much effort. You are likely to find the same is true for alcohol, refined sugar, and other unhealthy things you put into your body.

You may find that you are starting to avoid eating, or drinking things that you previously knew were unhealthy, but were unable to stay away from. Now these things cause you to feel uncomfortable. This is an indication that you are evolving. This level of sensitivity can only be obtained once you are aware, not only of your body, but also of your deeper feelings. What is so exceptional about this is that your deeper feelings must be acceptable to you. If they were not, you probably would have stopped using the tools that have brought you this new sensitivity. Congratulations, you have obtained peace of mind.

Another result of this increased sensitivity is that you may find engaging in a heated discussion or watching a violent TV show most upsetting. If this change occurs, it will be the result of a realization that these things damage your peace of mind. You have not only obtained peace of mind, but you have also learned to love it.

If you have learned to love your life, you will find that there is rarely enough time to do all the things you have learned to love. The value of using intuition to make decisions is not just the increase in decision-making accuracy, but also the time you save by not having to analyze facts ad nauseum. After a few months you can experiment with reducing the procedure for making decisions with your intuition and save even more time. It may no longer be necessary to match the exact feeling of the successful outcome of the event you are making a decision about. When waiting to detect a crink or a sum, you can simply monitor a feeling of general well-being and keep the golden light on. I recommend this shortcut only for simple things like cooking. Use a full procedure for more important decisions.

Synopsis

In this book you have been offered many different ideas. Some may help you to achieve peace of mind and others may inspire you to examine your values and beliefs. If either occurs, you will have a positive effect on yourself and those around you. If you decide to continue with the visualizations and tools presented in this book until using them becomes second nature, you will increase your ability to achieve the things you would love. And, if you only want to take a few ideas from the many that have been offered in this book (that's how I usually am), consider the three ideas below. As you continue along whatever road you choose, you will find that they can make your journey a pleasant one.

1. Do everything you enjoy in Present Time.
2. Stay in Center of Mind whenever you want to do your best.
3. Spend time loving your dreams.

If you have a problem that you feel is impossible, remember that many problems seem impossible until the solution reveals itself. For example, two evil brothers became prosperous through their evil ways. In their old age they desired respectability. They joined the church and contributed to charities. When the older brother died, the younger brother held out a check to the Priest who was to perform the funeral service, and said, "You can have $5,000 for your new school if you say that my brother was a saint." The Priest had a real dilemma on his hands, he had run out of money and the workers hadn't been paid for two weeks. But, he believed that all problems have a solution. So he took the check. During the funeral when it came time for the Priest to say a few words of his own, he told of all the bad things the older brother had done, "He was an evil man, he beat his dog, he cheated on his wife, but compared to his younger brother, he was a saint."

Appendix A – Hypnotic Induction

This induction is designed to be read to you by a friend. When selecting the person to read the induction, consider that the words need to be drawn out and held longer than normal speech. A person with a good singing voice can do this well. The first task is to have the reader develop the right voice tone, rhythm, and reading speed for the induction that you decide to use. This is not difficult because almost everybody knows how to say one set of words in the correct hypnotic voice. These are the words that people use to imitate a hypnotist. Those words are: you are feeling sleepy, soo sleeeeepy. The trick is to keep in mind how this phrase is said and continue talking in this manner. Introduce a slight, slow rhythm to your speech that adds monotony to the droning words. Consider doing some physical exercise to warm up the throat and vocal cords just before reading.

Customize the following induction to meet your needs and match your personality. At the designated place after the induction, insert the suggestions that you will develop from Appendix B. If there are any images that are not pleasant or relevant, another image can be substituted. You can use any book on hypnosis to aid you in developing different suggestions. The following induction refers to "a special place". This term should be replaced by the name of or the description of the most peaceful and secure place you can think of. It can be an imaginary place or somewhere you remember fondly. The most important requirement is that you can imagine yourself there alone and feel perfectly secure. The text of the following induction should be modified in the area that mentions the special place such that it makes grammatical sense depending on your special place, *in* the mountains, *at* the beach etc. Add as many details as you can. Have the person who is going to read the induction into the tape recorder silently practice reading the induction and suggestions once or twice. Have them make the recording alone.

The Induction

After you have filled in all the blanks in this and the following section, start the tape recorder and have your friend read the following to the end of this appendix:

Let your eyes remain lightly closed. Take a nice, deep breath and begin to relax. Just think about relaxing every muscle in your body from the top of your head to the tips of your toes. Just begin to relax and begin to notice how very comfortable your body is beginning to feel. You are completely supported, so you can just let go and relax.

Inhale and exhale. Feel the air filling your lungs and flowing out; in and out, in and out. And every time you exhale, release any tension, any stress from any part of your body, mind or spirit. Just let that stress go. Be aware of any stressful thoughts in your mind and feel them begin to wind down, wind down, wind down and relax.

Begin with letting all the muscles in your face relax, especially your jaw. Let your teeth part just a little and relax all the muscles around your jaw. And feel that relaxation spread across your face and relax all the muscles in your face. Feel your temples and forehead relax more and more. And now relax your eyes. Just imagine your eyelids feeling so comfortable, so heavy, so heavy, so relaxed. Continue to relax and feel all the muscles in your face relax. Relax more and more.

Every time you think about relaxing any area you will be able to feel those muscles relax even more. And as you exhale feel your stomach and chest muscles relax deeply, deeply relaxed.

Continue by relaxing all of the muscles in your neck and shoulders. On your shoulders feel a heavy weight gently pushing down, stretching the muscles in your neck and it feels good and more relaxed. And feel that soothing relaxation slowly move down your back, down, down, down to the lower part of your back, and all those muscles begin to relax, more and more relaxed.

Relax all of the muscles in your arms, from your shoulders down, down, down to your fingertips. Feel those muscles relax. And let your arms feel so heavy, so heavy, so relaxed. You may have tingling in your fingertips. That's perfectly fine. You may have warmth in the palms of you hands, and that's fine. And you may feel that you can barely lift your arms, they are so relaxed, they are so heavy, so heavy, so relaxed.

And down in your legs, let all the muscles in your legs relax, right to the tips of your toes. Let your muscles go. Feel them relax. Relax more and more. And inhale once again and relax your chest muscles. And as you exhale, feel your stomach muscles relax. More and more relaxed.

Notice how very comfortable your body feels. Just drifting and floating, deeper, deeper, deeper relaxed. And imagine that you are in an old hotel room. It is off season and the hotel is almost empty. You are on the tenth floor. It is early morning. The sun has been shining through your room making it warm and cozy. You have decided to go for a walk. Walk out of the room and down the hall to the open grill elevator. There is an elegant couch in the elevator. You sit on the couch. As I count from 10 to one you will drift past each floor. With each number you will drift down deeper, down deeper inside yourself. And with each number you will feel your body relax more and more.

The elevator starts very smoothly, ten... see the floors drift past as you float down deeper, down deeper, nine... floating down through the hotel, relaxing even more and more, eight... floating down, down, deeper down, deeper, seven... feel yourself float down deeper, down deeper, six... deeper, floating down deeper, deeper, five... floating down, relaxing deeper, deeper, four... down, down deeper, three... floating deeper, deeper, relaxing deeper, two... down, down, floating down, one... deeper, deeper, deeper relaxed.

The elevator smoothly stops. The door opens and you walk across the elegant lobby. It is early. There is no one around. The rug feels silky under your bare feet. You go outside and find a path through the woods. The path has fine sand and it feels cool on your feet. As you walk along the path you notice the plants along the path, the underbrush and the trees. You see the blue sky between the branches overhead and smell the fresh air. The woods are cool and inviting. The path starts to descend and gets steeper. Soon you come upon ten stairs leading down. But these stairs are special. You know that you will be able to flow down these stairs as if gravity had only one tenth its normal pull. You start to go down the stairs as I count from 10 to one, and with each step you drift deeper down inside yourself, deeper and more relaxed. Ten, nine, eight,

seven, six, five, four, three, two, one. At the bottom of the stairs you realize that this path leads to your special place in/by the _____. You walk down the path. Feel the ground under your feet. See the trees and underbrush on the side of the path. You have arrived in your special place on/in the _____. See your special place and feel its atmosphere, its peace. You see _____
_____ _____ (describe some features of your special place). Sit/lay down on/in the _____. You are alone and there is no one to disturb you. This is the most peaceful place in the world for you.

Imagine yourself in your special place and feel that sense of peace flow through you and feel a sense of well-being build up inside you. Enjoy these positive feelings and keep them with you long after this session is completed, for the rest of this day, and tomorrow. Allow these positive feelings to grow stronger and stronger, feeling at peace with a sense of well-being. And each and every time that you choose to do this kind of relaxation, you will be able to relax deeper and deeper. Regardless of the stress and tension that may surround your life, you will now remain more at peace, more calm, more relaxed, and allow the tension and stresses to bounce off and away from you, just bounce off and away from you.

Add Your Suggestions Developed in Appendix B Here

Look around and enjoy your special place on/in the _____ for a few moments and then I will begin to bring you back. (5 second Pause) It is time to come back up. Walk back along the path to where the stairs are. As I count from one to ten you will go back up the stairs. As you go up you will start to see a golden sun through the tree branches and you will begin coming back to full consciousness with each number. You will come back feeling refreshed, relaxed, and alert, as if you had a long rest. Come back feeling alert and relaxed. Begin to come back now. One..., two..., coming up, three..., four..., see the golden light, five..., six..., you see blue sky, seven..., the golden light is pouring through you, eight..., the golden light is filling you with energy, nine..., begin to open your eyes, and ten, open your eyes and come all the way back, feeling great, feeling refreshed and rested.

Appendix B – Hypnotic Suggestions

Chose three of the following eight suggestions and customize them for the recording of your hypnotic induction by adding specific information. Repetition is helpful; two or three repetitions of an important phrase can reinforce the idea and keep the person hypnotized. Also, every suggestion should be followed by instructions to create an image of the successful outcome.

The Successful Outcome Image for all Suggestions

And now see an image of yourself. You are happy and content you have completed the _____ project (solved the problem or accomplished your goal) and it feels good. You have completed the _____ project (solved the problem or accomplished your goal) on time and you feel very good. See yourself and after you have completed the _____ project (solved the problem or accomplished your goal) and feel the satisfaction, the joy, of this image.

Eight Typical Suggestions

Pick two or three of the following suggestions and customize them to your needs.

1) Present Time

Whenever you have a few spare moments, you will remember to practice Present Time and _____ (one of the other intuition practices). You choose to practice Present Time and _____ and it feels good. It feels very good. Picture yourself walking down a hall at work, you remember to do Present Time and _____ and you choose to do them. See yourself driving your car, you remember to do Present Time and _____ and you do them. And that feels very good, that feels very good.

2) Success

From now on, every day, you will do everything reasonable to make the _____ project a success. You will feel a strong desire to work on the _____ project and you will feel a strong desire to work on the most effective tasks to make the project a success. You will do everything necessary to complete the _____ project in a short time.

3) Work Reminder

From now on, whenever you have ten minutes you will work on the _____ project. Whenever you have a spare ten minutes you will remember to work on the _____ project. Whenever you have a spare ten minutes you will feel a strong desire to work on the _____ project.

4) Love and Respect

You are a likable person, you are a lovable person, and there are people who would like to know you and who would love you. Feel what it would be like to meet and get to know these people. (pause five seconds) Allow this feeling to grow inside of you today, tomorrow and each and every day. These people are your soon to be friends, your new lover. They respect and care for you. Feel that respect and caring coming from them. Soon you will find the right people, the people who will love you, and it feels very good.

5) Stress

From now on your subconscious will monitor your shoulders and neck muscles. You will notice whenever tension has raised your shoulders and you will remember to drop your shoulders and relax. Whenever tension raises your shoulders you will remember to drop your shoulders and relax. And now see yourself working in a relaxed and balanced state. Your breathe deeply and every breath allows your tension to flow out of your body. Even the slightest amount of tension is released before it has a chance to develop. And every time that tension starts to enter your body you will take a deep breath, drop your shoulders and relax.

6) Substituting Desires

It can take a little practice but it is not difficult to imagine what it feels like to be thirsty or hungry. Once you have imagined how it feels to have these desires for food or drink it is possible to feel this desire on command and to actually generate any desire that you might normally have. The following suggestions take advantage of this ability and turn it into a powerful tool for motivation.

7) Losing Weight

It is after 6:00 in the evening. You see your kitchen as you walk towards it. And now you see your refrigerator. As you see your refrigerator you feel a strong desire to get a drink of water. See the refrigerator now and feel the strong desire to get a drink of water. You go and get a drink of water and it satisfies you completely. You are completely satisfied. See yourself with the water. Feel the satisfaction of having drunk the water instead of eating the food you know you don't need or want.

8) Getting to the Gym

It is after work and you are driving home. You come to the crucial intersection. To the right is home. To the left is the gym and a good workout. See the intersection in your mind's eye from the driver's seat of your car. As you see the intersection, feel the strong desire to go to the gym. See the intersection and feel the desire to work out. You remember how good it feels to work out. You go to the gym and that feels so good. That feels so good. See yourself going to the gym and feel that good satisfaction, that feeling of accomplishment. Feel proud and healthy.

How Suggestions Work

The reason why these suggestions work well is that the subconscious does not get lost in the activity of the present like the conscious mind does. It is therefore in a better position to remind a person to do something. Also, the subconscious is more suggestible than the conscious mind. If the subconscious mind is told that there will be a strong desire to do something, that strong desire will be felt. It is also a good idea to include a date for completion or resolution of the task. The subconscious needs a target date just as much as the conscious mind or else tomorrow will always be soon enough to work on the problem.

In suggestion #2, a powerful element is present that you may want to include in all of the other suggestions. Suggestion #2 is actually calling upon your intuition to make a selection, the most effective task. Hypnotic suggestions are an excellent way to make use of your intuition because the subconscious is in close contact with a person's intuition. When a person under hypnosis is told that they will feel a strong desire to work on the most effective tasks their subconscious will access their intuition to discover the most efficient tasks. Such a suggestion would simply state that you will make the best decisions or selections to accomplish the desired outcome.

Considerations for Best Effect

Follow these suggestions for the most effective hypnotic sessions.

When To Use the Tape

The best time to listen to the tape will depend on how easily you fall asleep. Most people transit through a light trance as they fall asleep. However, you do not want to fall completely asleep when listening to the tape. If you take a long time to fall asleep, you can listen to the tape just before you go to bed or even in bed. If you fall asleep quickly and easily you should listen to the tape at a time when you would normally not fall asleep.

Preparation

Insure that your body is free from drugs that might cause you to be stimulated or distracted. Make yourself feel as relaxed as possible. Relaxation is the key to a good hypnosis session. Take off your shoes, loosen any tight clothing, and stretch a couple of times. Deep, relaxed breathing is important so make sure that your clothes do not restrict your diaphragm. The best position to try first is lying on your back with your head and shoulders slightly elevated.

Noise

During the session you may hear noises that ask for your attention. These noises can actually be used to push you deeper inside yourself, which is the aim of hypnosis. Allow them to be there and let them push you deeper into your relaxation. If you feel an itch, scratch it. If you get uncomfortable, shift your position. If you want to laugh or cry, feel free to do so. Both are releasing actions that will help you to achieve deeper relaxation.

Use headphones. A voice that is coming from right next to your ear commands much more attention than a voice coming from a few feet away.

Concentration

It's OK to daydream during the tape. It can actually help to bring you deeper if you engage in that free association that is normally experienced just before falling asleep. However, if you find yourself worrying about problems or making plans, gently bring yourself back to the sound of the voice. This is a time to put your problems aside and enjoy the pleasure of total relaxation. If you consciously realize that you can't remember what was just said, that is perfectly fine. Just gently return to the sound of the voice. You don't need to remember or understand. Only your subconscious needs to hear the tape and it will if you are not deeply asleep.

Falling Asleep

It is a good idea to record a "wake up" segment on the tape about 20 seconds after the hypnosis session is finished. Use your own voice. If you did not wake up some time between the "count back up" and this wake up portion, then you were too deep. You need to make changes to ensure that you do not fall asleep. You can change your position to sitting up straighter or change the time of day when you listen to the tape. Most people are very sleepy around 3:00 and may go too deep at this time. The time you normally go to sleep is another time to avoid if you find that you are going too deep.

Not Deep Enough

If you feel that you did not obtain even a light trance (usually indicated by a feeling of heaviness in your arms or legs), perform a few minutes of relaxation (similar to what is done on the tape) just before turning on the tape, and/or listen to the tape near bed time or around 3:00 P.M. (the middle time between waking and going to sleep). You can try laying down completely, covering up with a comfortable blanket, drinking something warm (no sugar or caffeine), or any other activity which you know helps you to relax.

Schedule

For the first week try to listen to the tape everyday. During the second week listen to the tape every other day. Thereafter, pick two days a week, e.g., Monday and Thursday, to listen to the tape. If at anytime you feel that you did not get a good session, listen to the tape the very next day.

Effectiveness

Sometimes there are no physical sensations or lapses of memory to indicate your hypnotic state. This often indicates that you have a good connection between your subconscious and conscious minds. Lucky you. Do not concern yourself with wondering if you were really hypnotized. That is almost exactly like wondering if you were really dreaming or just daydreaming. Continue to practice hypnosis for a couple of weeks. If you are getting to your subconscious, the effects will present themselves by the end of this period. At the very least you will have experienced a greatly reduced stress level. Even if you learn that you are not hypnotizable, you will have learned how to help people through hypnosis. It is such an effective method to help just about any situation that I am surprised that half the people in the world do not hypnotize the other and then trade places.

Printed in the United States
1007400001B